Being Catholic

A user's guide

D0927168

Being Catholic

A user's guide

A publication of the National Religious Vocation Conference

VISION
VOCATION GUIDE
WWW.VOCATIONGUIDE.ORG

Introduction

E ACH GENERATION of Catholics comes to define for itself what it means to be followers of Christ. The faith has been handed down from our parents and grandparents, our mentors and friends. But only when we make it our own does the Gospel—the radical, wild, wholly unexpected good news of Jesus—fill our hearts and shape our lives.

At the same time, Christian traditions vary, as do individual expressions of Christianity, and sometimes it is difficult to understand all the subtle distinctions. With the goal of helping Catholics mine the profound riches of our tradition, we introduced "Being Catholic" in the annual VISION Vocation Guide and invited respected Catholic writers to offer their insights into what it means to be Catholic. The compilation presented here represents a wide-ranging showcase of lived Catholicism and applied Christianity—from understanding the Creed to praying with scripture to caring for the poor to singing at Mass.

"With Christ joy is constantly born anew," says Pope Francis in *Evangelii Gaudium*, "The Joy of the Gospel," his 2013 apostolic exhortation to the community of faith. We hope that our slim volume will instill newfound joy in its readers as it highlights the many good reasons for cherishing, practicing, and celebrating your Catholic identity.

Most of all we hope that *Being Catholic: A User's Guide* will help the current generation of Catholics understand that the church is or can be "a place of mercy freely given, where everyone can feel welcomed, loved, forgiven, and encouraged to live the good life of the Gospel" *(Evangelii Gaudium)*. We want all Catholics to know that they can be proud of their faith, that it can give deep meaning and purpose to their lives, and that they can feel confident to call others into the saving love of Jesus.

And thus may the legacy and blessings of faith continue with the good news being proclaimed from generation to generation!

—Patrice J. Tuohy
Executive Editor, VISION Vocation Guide
Publisher, TrueQuest Communications

Ten great things about being Catholic

By Alice Camille

Some may settle for a baptism, wedding, and funeral in the church and feel they've gotten the best. But if you choose to live all the moments in between from the perspective of the Catholic worldview, you can enhance your life beyond your wildest imaginings.

WERE YOU BAPTIZED AS A BABY? If you're like most Catholics, that's how you first joined the church. Infant baptism has its obvious advantages: the early vaccination against original sin, guaranteed new life in Christ, and membership in the church—all nothing to sneeze at. But there's one drawback to starting your life as a Catholic while you're still in diapers: You have no idea what you're getting into! In this respect, infant baptism might seem to have all the charm of being drafted. If you happen to meet the criteria—in most cases, just having Catholic parents—you're in.

Embracing a Catholic identity, however, is a whole lot more than simply being a card-carrying member of the church. Some may settle for a baptism, wedding, and funeral in the church and feel they've gotten the best of it. But if you choose to live all the moments in between from the perspective of the Catholic worldview, you can enhance your life beyond your wildest imaginings.

What follows are 10 good things to discover for yourself about the beauty and integrity of authentic Catholic living. See how many of these windows of grace are open to you already, and how many more you may have to explore. You may also want to add to this list the things about the church that move you to awe and wonder.

1. We brake for mystery

The word *mystery* has a particular meaning in pop culture. We may think immediately of detectives trying to solve crimes, or suspenseful movies with some monster hiding in wait for its next victim. Our basic assumption about mystery is that it's something to be uncovered or resolved.

But the larger and more religious sense of mystery is of something that cannot be solved by human reason or even perceived by human senses.

This is our first understanding of who God is—a Being infinite, eternal, and essentially unknowable by limited mortal minds. We can ponder religious mysteries but never come to the end of them. So we meditate on how God becomes a human being, how a virgin can be a mother, how a crucified man rises from the dead, or how one day, the last will be first.

2. God's story is our story

For all Christians, the Bible is the foundation of our faith. But it's not a history book about how the world came to be, or stories of people from long ago. We believe God's Word is alive, that these stories are bigger than history and truer than a mere retelling of the past. Catholics don't look to the Bible to explain or replace scientific knowledge about the world. We accept these stories as the way ancient people shared what they were learning about the God who was leading them to become more fully human. They came to believe that the story of God is also the story of humanity, because our origin and life is in God. When we read the Bible, we find our own story written in its pages.

3. There's no cosmic even-steven

Without scripture, we might be forced into considering two rather distressing ideas about reality as we know it. One is that things happen in a random way and nothing matters or has meaning. As hard as that sounds, the other idea is equally unhappy: that God is handing out rewards and punishments according to a scale of justice that is coldly precise. Who among us wants to face perfect justice? But according to salvation history—another name for God's plan as the Bible illustrates it—God's desire is to save us, not to condemn us. Because we're not good enough to face even-steven justice, God chooses to exercise mercy instead. If we seek God's mercy, our sins are forgiven. This is why we call the gospel the "good news"!

4. In the common we find the holy

We have said God is unknowable, but that's not the end of the story. God is beyond our comprehension, but God wants to be known by us. God created us out of love, and love always seeks to be closer to the beloved. So God reveals the divine presence and purpose to the people of the Bible, folks like ourselves—part saint and part sinner.

God also expresses the divine will in the ancient law of the Old Testament. Finally, God enters human history directly through the person of Jesus, who is Son of God and one with God in a unique way. In turn, Jesus gives us an enduring way to encounter his presence in what the church now calls the sacraments. In common things—water, oil, bread, wine, words, touch, a ring, a promise—we meet the holy presence of God once more.

5. Many roads lead to prayer

Prayer is primarily communication, and there are countless ways to do it. Some pray in silence, mindful of God's presence. Others like to sing—Saint Augustine called singing "praying twice." Some find themselves naturally drawn to formal prayers of repetition like the Rosary or novenas. The Stations of the Cross, a walking prayer, reminds us that we're all pilgrims on a spiritual journey toward our true home. Group prayer is often made simpler by using a ritual like the Liturgy of the Hours, also known as the breviary. The ultimate prayer of the Catholic community is the Mass itself, in which we celebrate the central mysteries of our faith: "Christ has died, Christ is risen, Christ will come again!"

6. We have found the church, and it is us

The word *church* is remarkably broad. We use it to describe a building in which we worship. But it also refers to an authority that governs us—for Catholics, that usually means the Vatican, the bishops or other clergy, or the general body of people who are on the payroll of a parish office. Because we often speak of the church as something or someone "out there," we have to consciously remind ourselves that we are the church, the Body of Christ. We are called by God and empowered through the gifts of the Holy Spirit to carry the presence of Christ into the world today. You take "church" with you wherever you go!

7. The body has many parts

All who are baptized are known as the "People of God," according to church teaching. The People of God have a noble vocation to live out that identity with dignity and integrity. We are supported in that calling through the service of our church leaders—the pope who governs and coordinates the worldwide church; the college of cardinals who oversee broad territories; the bishops in their teaching office in each diocese; and the pastors guiding each parish. Add to their service the work of religious sisters and brothers, monks and cloistered nuns, missionaries, lay leaders and teachers, dedicated parents,

and countless organizations affiliated with the church. All together, we are the
hands and feet, the eyes and ears and voice of Christ in the world today.

8. We hold a treasure old and new

Some Christian churches maintain that the Bible alone teaches us the will
of God for the world. Catholics believe that the Bible is fundamental in
revealing God's purposes—and that God has made other revelations that are
also compelling. Creation is God's first and largest self-expression, for God
spoke the world into being and then created humanity in the divine image
and likeness.

Since Jesus told his disciples to "go forth, baptize, and teach all nations,"
Catholics also view the church itself as having a role to play in expressing
God's will in the world. The teaching authority of the church, known as the
magisterium, seeks to express God's hopes for humanity in every new generation.

9. Church is a verb

We mentioned that "church" is not just a building but also a people. More
perfectly understood, church is also something we do and not just who we
are. Our vocation to "be" church engages us with a world in crying need
of the presence of Christ. And Jesus wasn't just present to people; he came
to town and got to work teaching, healing, blessing, and giving hope to the
hopeless. He spoke out in defense of the poor, the suffering, and the excluded.
When we involve ourselves in works of justice, working to right the imbal-
ance of power in the world, we are "being church" most profoundly.

10. We live as we believe

Being human naturally means making moral choices. It might seem hard
at times, but it's not rocket science. A Catholic morality is shaped by many
principles, including the idea that human life belongs to God and not to us.
This is why we take a moral stand away from abortion, capital punishment,
euthanasia, genetic engineering, and all avoidable warfare. It's also why we
support fidelity in marriage, the welfare of children, and public policies that
lead to justice and peace. As Jesus put it succinctly, "Love one another." It's
still the best moral advice there is.

The Creed: A force to be reckoned with

By Patrice J. Tuohy

The Creed took centuries to develop and will take more than the lifetime of each believer to fully comprehend, but its main truth is disarmingly simple: You are loved.

IN THE FIRST EPISODE OF *STAR WARS*, the good Princess Leia is being held captive on the Death Star by Darth Vader and the bad Empire forces, who threaten to blow up her home star if she doesn't tell them where a rebel outpost is. Even though she gives them information (albeit false), the bad guys blow up her home anyway. At the very moment the star is blown up, Obi-Wan Kenobi, the wise old Jedi master, who is working with Luke Skywalker, Han Solo, and R2-D2 to rescue Princess Leia, nearly faints. When he regains composure, he says, "I felt a great disturbance of the force as if thousands of voices screamed out and were suddenly silenced."

Imagine the surge of energy Obi Wan Kenobi would sense from the strength of millions of voices calling out not in death but in life. That is the power of the Creed recited at every Mass and varied Christian liturgies in every corner of the globe, any day of the week. The force of close to a billion voices is with them each time Christians pray these words:

I believe in one God,
the Father almighty,
maker of heaven and earth,
of all things visible and invisible.

I believe in one Lord Jesus Christ,
the Only Begotten Son of God,
born of the Father before all ages.
God from God, Light from Light,
true God from true God, begotten, not made, consubstantial
with the Father;
through him all things were made.
For us men and for our salvation
he came down from heaven,

and by the Holy Spirit was incarnate of the Virgin Mary,
and became man.
For our sake he was crucified under Pontius Pilate,
he suffered death and was buried,
and rose again on the third day
in accordance with the Scriptures.
He ascended into heaven
and is seated at the right hand of the Father.
He will come again in glory
to judge the living and the dead
and his kingdom will have no end.

I believe in the Holy Spirit, the Lord, the giver of life,
who proceeds from the Father and the Son,
who with the Father and the Son is adored and glorified,
who has spoken through the prophets.

I believe in one, holy, catholic and apostolic Church.
I confess one Baptism for the forgiveness of sins
and I look forward to the resurrection of the dead
and the life of the world to come.

Amen.

In other words

Most Christians can recite these words (or a previous version of the Creed) by heart, but many of us might stumble if we actually had to explain the meaning behind this compact statement of belief.

The Nicene Creed, which is the creed Catholics recite at Mass, was initially formulated at the Council of Nicea (in modern Turkey) in 325 and completed in 381 at the Council of Constantinople. Its main concern was to counter the Arian heresy, which denied the full divinity of Jesus and the triune nature of God.

Thus, in the Creed we state our belief in one God, the Father. In Jesus Christ, who is "consubstantial with the father," and the Holy Spirit, "who proceeds from the Father and the Son."

The members of the Council were particularly concerned with anticipating any loopholes that would allow unorthodox teachings to prevail, so they included extensive descriptions of Jesus: the only Son of God, born of the Father before all ages . . . God from God . . .

Saint Athanasius, who played a key role at the Council, is credited with the beautiful image of Jesus as Light from Light, true God from true God, which draws from an analogy common among Athanasius and his followers that compared God to the sun and Jesus to the sun's rays. The argument went something like this: The sun's rays are derived from the sun (not vice versa), but there was never a time when the sun existed without its light. So, too, Jesus exists through the Father but there was never a time when the Father existed without the Son. Thus, they argued God and Jesus are co-eternal, and Jesus is, as we say in the Creed, "true God from true God."

We believe, too, that the Holy Spirit proceeds from the Father and Son (this line is a sticking point for Orthodox Christians, who insist that the Spirit proceeds from the Father alone—but that is another day's argument).

Mainly we believe that our God is Father, Son, Spirit, or said another way: Our God is Creator, Redeemer, and Sanctifier of all life. All that exists comes through this triune God. That is why we believe creation is ultimately good, and all God's creatures are worthy of dignity and respect.

Finally, we believe that the church, the community of faithful, is one (united), holy (of God) catholic (universal, encompassing all the local churches), and apostolic (active and communal). In other words we believe that to be Christian is not just to follow a set of rules or adhere to a set of beliefs; being Christian by its very nature means being part of a community that traces its roots to the earliest Christian communities. It means sharing God's word, breaking bread together, and living out the gospel in fellowship with others.

You are loved

The Creed took centuries to develop and will take more than the lifetime of each believer to fully comprehend, but its main truth is disarmingly simple: You are loved. You were created out of love, your life's purpose is to love and be loved, and nothing can separate you from your one true love, who is eternal, real, steadfast, and ever-present.

The details of how that love gets expressed are unique to each believer—some may choose to live their lives in service to the poor; others to fight social injustice; still others to teach and offer counsel. Some may choose to commit to a celibate lifestyle and live in a religious community while others may choose different forms of consecrated life, Holy Orders, Matrimony, or single life. All ways are holy, yet not all ways are right for each of us. Our main purpose as Christians is to find the best way to live out God's call to love.

Our path is not always apparent, but we are not without help along the way. We have the church, consisting of the community of faithful, the magisterium (the pope, cardinals, bishops, and so on who make up the teaching church), scripture, and tradition, all of which point to the many ways people throughout salvation history have accepted and expressed God's love. We also have God in the person of Father, Son, and Spirit continually drawing us into Divine goodness.

Live joyfully

One thing is certain: No matter which way we turn, no matter where we put our focus and energy and commitments, our lives should lead to joy—deep, satisfying, life-giving joy. Confusion and doubt are part of the process, even a little anguish and sense of loss for the paths we could have taken, but our overriding spiritual and emotional state should be one of joy as we journey toward God.

We are part of the light of the world—this light is our origin and destination. Though our lives will contain many sorrows, Christians are not a sorrowful people. We are God's children, not his crabby, fretful next-door neighbors. God expects us to delight in life. A look at the holiest people in history or in your own backyard gives witness to this delight. "Cheerfulness strengthens the heart and makes us persevere in a good life," said Saint Philip Neri, known as the "Saint of Joy." "Therefore the servant of God ought always to be in good spirits."

So when you find yourself at a crossroad, at a time of major decision and transition, instead of succumbing to angst and fear, it is wise to go back to the basics, just as a golfer breaks down the elements of his swing or a ball player goes over the fundamentals of the game. Try reciting the Creed and remind yourself of the core beliefs of Catholic faith that tell you why you are here (because God created you out of love) and what your purpose is (to give and receive love). Most of all remember that you are not alone. A billion other souls are on a similar spiritual journey. Together we generate a powerful force of love. May the force be with you.

What Catholics believe about Jesus

BY FATHER PAUL BOUDREAU

Son of God, a human being, a healer, one who gave his life for the world and is present with us today—all these and more answer the question: Who is Jesus?

I N THE NAME OF THE FATHER, and of the Son . . . ." Wait! Hold it right there. What do you mean, the "Son"? Who is the Son? Who is this Jesus, whose name we use so freely, whose image shows up on bumper stickers, hangs on our walls, and even dangles from our ears? What do Catholics believe about this Jesus?

Truly God, truly human

He's the Son *of God* of course. And in that designation "Son" is wrapped up a world of meaning.

First, Jesus is the full and complete revelation of God. Jesus makes the invisible God visible to us and real in a way we can access and engage. To be truly the Son of God, Jesus was conceived by the Holy Spirit, the only begotten of the Father. That is important so we can understand that Jesus wasn't our idea; he was God's. God, out of love for us, made it happen.

Jesus is also the "Son of Man." God is a mystery beyond our understanding but Jesus is one of us, born of a woman, like us in flesh and blood. Jesus knew what it was like to be a human being, to suffer weakness and temptation, to hunger, to laugh and to cry, to love and to be afraid, to be frustrated, angry, happy, and hopeful. He knew wealth and poverty. He knew what it was like to grow up in a human family, to upset his parents, and to leave home and set out on his own. He knew acceptance and rejection. He even knew what it was like to suffer and die. Though he did not commit sins, he carried the burden of our sins and suffered the consequences of them. Jesus did it all for us.

The Nicene Creed wraps all this up by saying that Jesus is true God and true man. In other words, Jesus is God, through and through. There is no factor of divinity missing in Jesus. He always existed and always will exist. All things exist through him, with him, and in him. He is the source of all that is, the beginning and the end of everything.

At the same time, Jesus is truly human. That means that even though he was, is, and always will be God, in a moment of time he entered history as a human being. Like all of us he was conceived, born, lived, loved, laughed, suffered, and died.

The Lamb of God

There is a kind of cosmic principle that governs life in this world that is expressed in various ways. For instance, we say, "What goes around, comes around" or "you reap what you sow." People sometimes use the term karma, common to Hinduism and Buddhism, a word that represents the natural, impersonal law of moral cause and effect found in the universe. Simply put, we say that you pay for your sins.

Well, Jesus picked up the tab. Whatever you did, said, or even thought that was wrong, Jesus took the hit for you. At Mass, we call Jesus the "Lamb of God who takes away the sins of the world." Jesus was accused, arrested, brought to trial, judged, condemned, and put to death. That about covers it for all of us who are guilty of sin.

To ancient people who made their living off their flocks, lambs were considered the most valuable possession of the tribe, their hope for the future. In an annual ritual, one of the lambs, supposedly the best one, was offered to God as a sacrifice to pay the price, the cosmic debt owed by the people. The lamb was offered for the forgiveness of sins.

Jesus is the Lamb of God offered for the forgiveness of our sins. Because it is God's offering, it is infinite. That means that the forgiveness won for us by the sacrifice of Jesus atones not only for our sins but the sins of all the world. That's everybody. No exceptions. It is also eternal. That's why in the Apostles' Creed we say Jesus "descended into hell" to spring all those who died in sin before the event of Jesus and were paying off their debt. The eternal redemption of Jesus reaches back to Adam and forward to the end of the world.

Jesus the healer

In the forgiveness of sins we also have healing, and Jesus is the healer. The gospel stories of Jesus link his many miracles of healing with forgiveness. Our sins, and the sins of all the world, bring about conflict and discord. When we sin, we set ourselves against the purpose for which we were created: to know, love, and serve God and to be happy with God forever. Sin, in other words, takes away our peace, our ease. Forgiveness restores peace to the soul, reconciles the person with the purpose, and sets the person once again on the path to fulfillment. Jesus is the Prince of Peace, the healer who reconciles humanity with God.

A sign of contradiction

When Mary and Joseph brought the infant Jesus to the Temple, the prophet Simeon referred to him as a "sign that will be contradicted." You figure anyone whose mother is a virgin would have to be somewhat of a contradiction! This contradiction is also seen in the proclamation of the kingdom of God. In it, Jesus says, the last shall be first and the first shall be last; the blind see, the lame walk, the deaf hear. Jesus is the dead man who lives, the source of life for all who die. He is the sinless Son of God who is judged by the world and condemned to death. He is the sign the world contradicts.

That is why Jesus calls his followers to "repent, for the kingdom of heaven is at hand." The word repent simply means "to turn around"; to change—good advice considering that the world and all that is in it is passing away, but the Kingdom is coming and it will endure forever. Take your pick: "What profit do you show," Jesus says, "if you gain the whole world and lose your own self?"

The Bread of Life

All of these aspects of who Jesus is are embodied in the Eucharist, the source and summit of sacramental life in the church. When we gather for Mass, Christ is made present in mystical ways.

He is made present in the assembly of the people. The Body of Christ is made up of its members, those who live through, with, and in Christ.

Christ is made present in the Word of God proclaimed and received by the assembly, for Jesus is the Word made flesh, the revelation of God. When God created the world, each day of creation brought forth a part of the world with a word: *be*. Let there *be* light; let there *be* a heaven and earth; let there *be* life. In the fullness of time, when the angel called upon the Virgin Mary to conceive and bear the Son of God, her response was, "Let it *be* done." And Jesus cured others with a word: "*Be* healed." On the cross, as he surrendered himself to death, Jesus proclaimed: "It *is* finished." Jesus is the total and complete revelation of God contained in all of the Bible, the Word of God, not only written on a page or spoken by a reader but embodied and lived by Jesus.

Jesus is also made present in the person of the priest who presides at the altar, the table of the Lord's sacrifice. The eternal reality of the Lord's Supper breaks into time at the Mass. As Jesus reclined at table with his disciples, so the priest stands at the table of the Lord's Supper with the faithful.

Jesus is the Bread of Life. He is present in the Eucharist; his Body and Blood are manifested under the appearance of bread and wine. In the celebration, the bread is offered and becomes his Body; the wine is offered and becomes his Blood. He is *Emmanuel*, "God with us." The mystery of faith is revealed: Christ has died, Christ is risen, Christ will come again.

The "come again" part is experienced in two ways. One is that Jesus will come again at the end of time. When that day comes, when our lives in this world end, Jesus will appear. "I will come back again," he said, "and take you to myself." He joins us in suffering and death so that we might join him in resurrection and glory. Halleluiah! Come Lord Jesus!

The other way is that Jesus comes all the time. As he comes in baptism to unite us with himself in dying and rising, and to wash us clean of our sins, so he comes to us again and again in the sacraments of the church. He is present in the power of the Holy Spirit that comes to us in the sacrament of Confirmation. The union of husband and wife is a sign of the union of Christ and the church.

In the sacrament of Reconciliation, we encounter Jesus who is the forgiveness of our sins. The person of the ordained minister becomes the person of Christ at the table of the Word of God and the sacrament of his Body and Blood. The Eucharist is itself the Real Presence of Christ among us and within us. In the end, we are anointed and are joined with Christ, the anointed one, in suffering and death. In both these experiences, Jesus is Christ and Messiah, the hope and expectation of all people for all time.

In union with Christ

All of the above is communion with Jesus. Everything we believe about Jesus is realized in the meal of his Body and Blood. We become what we eat. In that he has taken the form of our human existence, bearing the cross of our sins, suffering with us, even dying with us, so too we are invited to join him in the reality of his divinity. To the degree that we conform our thoughts, words, and actions to that of Jesus, then to that degree we are one with him. Jesus has done his part. It remains for us to do ours.

How to get the most out of scripture

BY STEVE MUELLER

The A-B-Cs of skillful Bible reading are building blocks to learning about yourself, your faith, and your relationship with God.

L IKE ANY OTHER SKILL, reading the Bible needs to be learned and developed through practice. Being a skillful Bible reader will depend on using good methods to discover the meaning of what you read. You need to recognize the words and understand their meaning so that you can apply the message to your life. Reading any text, especially an ancient one like the Bible, is always challenging.

One Bible, many meanings

As people discover when they share their biblical insights with family, friends, or faith-sharing groups, the meanings they discover in the Bible seem endless. One reason for this is that your mind can never fully grasp the divinely revealed mysteries about God. But the Bible *does* guide you and help you discover and understand your relationship with God. It also challenges you and calls into question who you are and how you live.

Another reason for so many different meanings is that as your reading situation and personal needs change, so will what you discover in the Bible. Being in a relationship with another is a never-ending surprise about both the other and yourself, so you must learn to live the Bible's questions and let them challenge you. When what you read makes you uncomfortable, you can be sure this is a sign from God about where you need to grow.

To become a more skillful Bible reader, it helps to have a handy method to go about your task of reading. One such approach makes it as easy as A-B-C! This technique focuses on the three basic steps of your reading.

1. Approaching the text

As readers, what you get out of a passage depends largely on what you bring to it. The written words are fixed on the page and everybody reads the same words but discovers many different meanings. Some of this dissimilarity arises from the personal differences in knowledge and experience that readers bring to their interpretation of the passage. Other differences arise from the interests that guide their reading and from the connections that they make to their lives.

Whenever you want to read the Bible, it helps to consider your personal assumptions by asking some basic questions about why you want to read the Bible:

- What is going on in my life that points me toward the Bible?
- Why would I want to read the Bible and not some other book?
- What do I want or expect to discover from this reading?
- What questions, concerns, or needs do I wish to address?
- What do I want to focus on now: the theological issue of who God is or how God acts; historical issues about when and where the events described happened; psychological issues about the motivations or values that prompt biblical persons' choices; the application to my own problems by seeing how the biblical story is my story? There is no end to what might interest you and focus your approach to the biblical passage.

2. Breaking open the text

Discovering the meaning of a biblical passage moves in two stages.

First, ask yourself *what the passage says* and then *what it means*. To understand what a biblical passage says you need to rely on an accurate modern translation like the New American Bible Revised Edition or the New Revised Standard Version (get the annotated versions with the helpful notes). Read the selected passage all the way through without looking at any footnotes or other material. Sit quietly with the reading for a minute, reflecting on it. If there are words or phrases or religious terms that are not clear, look them up in a dictionary. As a clue for determining meaning, notice also what type of writing it is—gospel, letter, historical book, wisdom book, prophecy, and so on. At the least, determine whether it is prose or poetry.

To understand what the passage means, you must first ask what the original author wanted the original audience to understand by these words. After all, this author was the one who put these words together to convey a meaning to someone. Getting at what the ancient author originally meant is not always easy because the passage was composed centuries ago in a culture and language that were very different from ours. So you mostly rely on scripture scholars to identify this original meaning. The introductions and footnotes in your Bible usually give this kind of information. Commentaries—like the *New Collegeville Bible Commentary* or the *New Jerome Biblical Commentary*—help when you have further questions.

Once you have a sense of what the passage meant to its author and its first readers, you can connect that meaning to similar situations and needs in your own life. Their story is your story, too.

3. Connecting the text

The goal of reading the Bible is ultimately to live your relationships with God and others in a fuller Christian way. Connecting the Bible's meaning with your life can occur at any point and in any way. One way to discover possible connections to your life is to focus specifically on the *people* or on the *story*.

If you focus on the people, then you seek to connect points between their ideas, feelings, values, and behavior as examples for your own. Every person you encounter in the Bible is in some way like you. The root of the similarity is that both they and you are involved in a relationship with God. Their example of how they worked out the details in order to live out that relationship provides some clues for how you can do so, too.

If you focus on the story, then you seek to connect points between the biblical story and your life story. The Bible is the story of people in relationship to God. The relationship moves through a pattern of invitation and call, hearing and response, faith commitment and covenant, community and shared responsibility; building the relationship; meeting the challenges of obligations and changing yourself because of the relationship; and accepting the cost of maintaining the relationship. Where are you in this dynamic process of relationship with God? What are the challenges and demands that the biblical passage opens to you? How does the biblical passage help you live more fully your relationship with God?

God's Word at work

As you use this A-B-C method to explore the Bible, you will notice that reading the Bible is like a conversation that involves a give-and-take by which you are changed. When you approach the passage, you are also approached by God through the words of the passage. As you break open the meaning of the passage, you are broken open by God's living Word to be transformed by your relationship. As you connect the passage to your life, you are connected more closely to God through the words that you read. As you work on God's Word, God's Word works on you.

For Bible reading, merely gaining an intellectual insight is never the end of the process. When you discover the meaning of the passage, you move from information to application and action. Your reading of scripture is never simply for ideas or information but for the formation of yourself as a Christian. Bible reading is for living in relationship with God.

Five steps to finding your vocation

BY BROTHER DAVID STEINDL-RAST, O.S.B.

It's as simple as ask, trust, stop, listen, and respond.

D ID YOU KNOW THAT THE WORD *VOCATION* is related to the term "vocal cords" and means "a calling"? More precisely it means spending your life doing what your innermost heart feels called to do. To follow a vocation means living your own unique life. That's of course what all of us would like to accomplish, but how shall we do it?

Start by asking people who are doing what they really love to do, "How did you get to where you are?" You'll find that many of them started by asking themselves some basic questions 1. What would I really like to do? 2. What am I good at doing or learning? 3. What opportunity is life offering me, right now, for doing what makes me come joyfully alive? Thus they started with themselves, with their own gifts and preferences.

1. Ask what makes you come alive

Does starting with yourself sound selfish to you? If so you are most likely concerned with serving the world. That is certainly a worthwhile goal, and a most important one. But do you have the right approach? Howard Thurman, an outstanding civil rights activist, author of *Jesus and the Disinherited*, and a mentor of Dr. Martin Luther King, Jr., gave this advice: "Don't ask what the world needs. Ask what makes you come alive, and go do it. Because what the world needs is people who have come alive."

So what is it that makes you come alive? Whatever your answer it will point toward that way of serving the world for which you are best suited. When you do that, you express your unique personality—with all your talents and all your limitations and shortcomings and your struggle to overcome them—which makes you who you are, and this uniqueness is what the world needs.

Maybe you have heard about Helen Keller or have seen the film about her, *The Miracle Worker*. Keller was born with a brilliant mind, but when she was not yet 2 years old she lost forever both her eyesight and hearing. In spite of that, and with the help of her gifted and dedicated teacher Anne Sullivan, she learned to speak and write. She also became the first blind and deaf student to earn a bachelor of arts degree, got married, and distinguished herself as a social activist, lecturer, and writer.

There were even great saints—John Vianney, for example—who struggled with school and found it extremely hard to study. They may have failed their exams, but they didn't give up, and in the end they changed the world by their love and courageous service.

Examples of this kind can help you see that even your challenges and the way you deal with them are part of coming alive and thus serving the world. Yet, examples are given us for inspiration, not for imitation. There is a Jewish story about a rabbi who wanted to imitate Abraham, the father of faith. "Make me like Abraham," he prayed, "make me like Abraham!" But God said to him—so the story says—"Look, I already have an Abraham. I want you." Anyone you admire has already played her or his part; now it is up to you to play your own.

When you think of coming alive and playing your part, the image of a jazz band may help you see it is not selfish at all. How the members of a band play will depend not only on their skill as musicians but on how well they listen to each other. That is where we come to the third question that people who found their true vocation had asked themselves. After they wondered "What would I really like to do?" and "What am I good at?" they listened to all the other players and asked, "What opportunity is life offering me—right now?"

2. Trust the opportunities life and God are offering

Once you know what gives your heart deep and lasting joy, go for it! Trust life to provide every moment with exactly what you need (this courageous trust is called *faith*). If you truly trust in life, you can let go of your wishful daydreams and open yourself to reality with all its surprises (this openness for surprise is called *hope*). Going forward with trust and openness is like shouting a joyful "yes!" into the strong wind of life that meets you. Suddenly you realize: We all belong together. Life is a network of mutual belonging (and your "yes" to belonging is called *love*).

We sometimes get that wrong; we think that faith means believing something. But that is *belief*. Faith is courageous trust in life—trust in that mysterious source of life and aliveness that is called "God." And often we confuse *hope* with *our* hopes. But our hopes are for things and events we imagine; hope is openness to the unimaginable, to surprise; in fact *surprise* is a good name for God because it doesn't box God in. Love, too, is often misunderstood; we tend to confuse it with preference. But what makes love be love is not preference but the sense of mutual belonging. And because everything in the universe belongs inseparably together with everything else, love in the full sense is your "yes" to limitless belonging—a "yes" that is expressed not by words but by the way we live.

To live in faith and hope and love means finding your true vocation. It means to experience life with trust and openness and an all-embracing "yes" and so to come alive with the divine life within you. In the biblical story of creation we are given a beautiful image: As human beings we come alive when God breathes life into us. To use an image closer to us, we are like so many different soap bubbles, all filled with one and the same divine life-breath. To remind myself of that I like to blow soap bubbles on my birthday every year. If you remember that truth, you look differently at others—and not only at others; you look differently at yourself and at your relationship to that source, fullness, and dynamism of life that we call God. Then you understand why Saint Paul said: "In him we live and move and have our being"(Acts 17:28).

Is there a simple method to put all this into practice? There is. But remember, simple doesn't mean easy; you'll have to give it all you have. The method has three parts: stop, listen, respond.

3. Stop

Stop, or you will zoom right past the opportunity life is offering you this very moment. Unless you learn to stop, you are driving on automatic. You need to build stop signs into your daily life. Before you open your eyes in the morning, before you put the key into the ignition, before you open your computer, these beginnings invite you to stop for a split second. So do moments when something makes you stop—a traffic light, a line at the checkout counter, or someone arriving late. Endings, too, make good stopping points: As you get up from table, close your book, or turn off the light, stop ever so briefly. By stopping, you practice faith: You trust that life, and the Giver of Life, has a message for you, an invitation.

4. Listen

And then you listen—with the ears of your heart. To what does life invite you, right now? Most of the time life invites you to enjoy—what you see, taste, smell, touch, or hear. Stopping and listening makes you come alive with all your senses. Otherwise you miss these pleasures by rushing past them. But sometimes life invites you to learn something—for instance patience (that's not so pleasant)—or to move beyond what you are used to (that can also be challenging). At other times life may invite you to share—your time, your experience, your resources—or to stand up and be counted or to clean up a mess. Whatever it might be it will always be surprising if you only listen deeply enough. For this kind of listening is an exercise in hope. It makes you more and more open for surprise.

5. Respond

The greatest surprise will be to discover how by stopping and listening you come to interact lovingly with others if you practice the next step and respond to life's invitation at a given moment. That response is an exercise in love, your lived "yes!" to belonging. It is your answer to a very personal calling, and it turns whatever you are doing into a vocation, your unique vocation—for no other person can listen and respond with your heart. The joy you will find on this path, no matter how rough it may be at times, will prove to you that it is the right path for you. Then you will realize what it means when Jesus says, "I have come that they may have life and have it to the full" (John 10:10).

Catholic social teaching: a guide

By Kevin Clarke

You shouldn't have to learn about Catholic social teaching on the streets—but that's not a bad place to start!

I T'S THE KIND OF SUBJECT not a lot of parents are comfortable talking over with their children. Sometimes even educators in the finest schools are unwilling to bring it up with their students, worried that even just talking about it could lead to all these, well, feelings that might actually lead their kids to do something.

I'm talking, of course, about Catholic social teaching (what did you think I was talking about?). While it would be great to learn about Catholic social teaching (CST) from your parents, your parish, or your school, unlike some other subjects you actually can learn about CST from the streets because that's where it may inspire you to spend a lot of time, picketing for debt relief in the Third World, more humane health care policies in the United States, or affordable housing programs that will mean decent shelter for people in your community.

A secret best not to keep

In the same way we use Catholic moral teaching to provide the foundation for our personal examination of conscience, Catholic social teaching offers Catholics a powerful critique of the social contradictions and failures that can trouble our culture, which is based in faith and scripture, not in political theory.

Catholic social teaching provides a parallel framework to support an examination of institutional, economic, or social conscience. CST helps us track down structural occasions of sin and offers practical, commonsense, but always compassionate guidelines for effecting change aimed at mitigating such "social sin" and doing a kind of civic penance for it. CST escapes easy political labeling intended to shut down debate on contemporary social questions. It asserts a passionate moral challenge to Catholics of every generation.

Some have called this nearly 120-year-old tradition the church's best kept-secret. Personally I don't think CST is best kept secret for even a moment longer. That's because for young people wondering how their faith can be relevant to their lives or the crushing social needs of our times, or suspecting that Christians might be called to do more than respond with charity to social inequities that lead to want among others, CST is often a shocking revelation. It can motivate them to struggle for social justice while it contributes to a deeper understanding of the radical implications of their Christian faith.

The history of a teaching

Beginning with Pope Leo XIII's encyclical *Rerum Novarum* in 1891, this teaching continued with 1931's *Quadragesimo Anno*, gathered steam during the cultural and political turmoil of the 1960s, and was neatly bookended by the late Pope John Paul II's *Centesimus Annus* in 1991. CST has been augmented by statements and pastoral letters from bishops' conferences and includes another encyclical from Pope John Paul II, *Evangelium Vitae,* in 1995. The social encyclicals, basically letters to the faithful issued by various popes, were typically composed during periods of great social upheaval when economic or historic currents were challenging the church to think beyond its institutional borders.

CST's founding encyclical, *Rerum Novarum*, for example, was intended as a message of hope and support to working people around the world during the late 19th century. At that time, appalling working conditions and economic exploitation encouraged radical political alternatives that not only threatened the established social order but also challenged the relevance of the church itself.

While *Rerum Novarum* called both capitalists and workers to accept their different roles in society, it also detailed a series of new rights and responsibilities in a justly ordered society and asserted the freedom of workers to form unions to defend their rights. Later social encyclicals likewise were attentive to the signs of their times, extending the understanding of a just economic order meant to serve people—and not the other way around (the U.S. Catholic Bishops' pastoral letter *Economic Justice for All*, Pope John XXIII's encyclical *Mater et Magistra*); building a new spiritual framework toward the establishment of true peace in the world (John XXIII, *Pacem in Terris*); or redefining the notion of "authentic development" during a time when Western technocrats offered a purely materialist "fix" for the problems of human deprivation in the developing world (Paul VI's *Populorum Progressio*).

CST calls Catholics to reevaluate societal realities with a keen eye to the status of the individual, the family, and the community of humankind. It implores us to protect the sanctity of all life and creation, calls us to pay particular attention to the plight of the poor among us, and asks us to act always in a spiritual and practical union with our neighbors, whether those neighbors live next door or on another continent.

CST: The basics

A few major themes capture the heart of CST's decades of instruction.

• CST recognizes the sanctity of all life and seeks to protect and promote the dignity of all people. The church's position of defending the unborn is well known; less known is its insistence that all life by definition is imbued with worth, that human dignity, a CST theme, must be safeguarded whether from the careless violence of conflict or the indifferent mechanisms of a soulless economic order.

• In keeping with its defense of human dignity, CST repeatedly comes to the aid of working people (even as it details their just obligations to their employers), demanding a "just wage" for workers, time off to allow for recreation and family life, and other basic rights. A just economic and political order seeks the common good of all citizens and deplores a system that reduces workers to mere economic cogs in a relentless machinery of production and profit.

• CST also stresses what it calls a "preferential option for the poor," meaning that the needs of the poorest and most vulnerable people are always considered the first obligation in a justly ordered society.

• CST expresses the church's understanding of and commitment to solidarity, the idea that we are all members of one human family, that we are our brothers' and sisters' keepers, whether those family members may be represented by people unable to pay for decent health care in our own society or people going hungry because a global economic structure starves them of affordable food halfway around the world.

• The CST-based concept of subsidiarity argues that social problems should be resolved at the lowest appropriate level of authority. This concept encourages the full participation of the individual in his or her political life as a complete expression of their humanity, but also compels that appropriate authority be brought to bear to respond to specific social dysfunction. So, you and I may work collectively to resolve a community problem, but we have to appeal to our elected representatives when we seek redress of a larger social problem like unemployment, global hunger, or affordable housing or health care.

• CST asserts the right of all people to what might be called the basic necessities of life: food and shelter, education and employment, health care and housing. Securing those basics affords people the opportunity to achieve the full expression of themselves as individuals, as family members, and as participants in their civic society. We also have a duty to assure these rights for others and the obligation to express these rights in fulfillment of our responsibilities to our families, to each other, and to the larger society.

• Participation, therefore, in the judicious creation of a just social order through the political process becomes a moral responsibility for Catholics. We are called to involve ourselves in the resolution of our own problems and our nation's, whether that means working on our local school boards, running for political office, or advocating for greater generosity in foreign aid at the national level.

Defending human dignity, protecting the poor, promoting the common good—CST expects much from us as Christians and citizens, but it asks no more than what our God-given talents, passion, and energy can offer. Don't wait another moment to learn about this rich and powerfully motivating tradition of justice.

Accept the gift of forgiveness

BY FATHER BRITTO M. BERCHMANS

The ideal Catholic parish is a community of disciples who seek to live the example of Jesus. Contrition, confession, forgiveness, and reconciliation—all part of the sacrament of Reconciliation—are key ingredients to living the Christian life. A parish priest offers insights into this often neglected sacrament and the gifts it brings.

SAINT PAUL wrote in his Letter to the Romans, "All have sinned and fall short of the glory of God" (Romans 3:23). We all need reconciliation and God's forgiveness, but how do we obtain it? Catholics have been given a special gift: the privilege to be able to participate in the sacrament of Reconciliation.

We are also given a guarantee that God will forgive us because Jesus gave the power to forgive sins to the church through the apostles. At the end of John's gospel Jesus says to the disciples after the Resurrection: "Receive the Holy Spirit. Whose sins you forgive are forgiven them, and whose sins you retain are retained" (John 20:22-23).

Reconciliation, though, is not only about reciting a list of sins but also looking at the direction of your life. In Confession you meet with the priest and have a conversation about the actions you have done or failed to do that have set you off course. When the priest eventually says, "Go in peace, change your life," you can go with the guarantee that things have been set aright. You can have that serenity and peace that you have been forgiven.

Why we neglect the sacrament of Reconciliation

Yet the sacrament of Reconciliation has fallen out of favor with many Catholics, and that is unfortunate. There are a number of reasons for that.

One reason is that people have lost the sense of sin. If you lose that, then you don't feel the need to go and ask for forgiveness. However, until you realize that you sin, conversion doesn't happen and you do not really grow in holiness.

A second reason is that people have lost the sense of the sacramentality of life—that God works through material signs—that reflect eternal truths. If you've lost the imperative to demonstrate outwardly what you say you believe and feel inwardly, then it's hard to see the purpose for sacraments like Reconciliation.

A third reason that Reconciliation has fallen out of favor is the sex abuse scandals and the way they were handled. Many people have lost faith in the priesthood and feel justified for not participating in a sacrament that they believe has been neglected by the very people who are commissioned to administer the sacrament.

Finally, we have become very this-worldly. Once upon a time there was a much deeper sense of heaven and hell and eternal destiny, but today people don't think much about it. We keep death and the ultimate consequences of our actions out of sight. If you are mindful of the divine and eternal, you live in a different way. People are so caught up with the busyness of everyday life that they lose sight of God's grand plan and our role in it.

Why go through the motions?

So given all the reasons for its neglect, just why should Catholics make the effort to participate in the sacrament of Reconciliation? The answer is simple: because you will feel better—physically, emotionally, and spiritually. The benefits are endless. But probably the most important is the spiritual benefit.

Sin is predominantly an act of pride. So forgiveness comes from the opposite: being humble. There is no greater act of humility than to say, "Bless me, Father, for I have sinned." And that brings about God's grace, and releases you from the bonds that come with trying to be the best, the greatest, the strongest, the most powerful, the most successful. Just going to Confession and acknowledging your prideful actions does something for you. No matter what the priest says or doesn't say, the act of acknowledging your false steps is a great act of humility.

And as Saint Augustine tells us, humility is the first (and the second and third) secret of holiness. To grow in holiness you need humility, and there is no better way to become humble than to go to Confession.

God gives us sacraments that on the surface look like external actions but also create an effect that is spiritual and internal. Just as when a man and a woman pronounce their vows before God and God's people, it is not only two people expressing their love for each other but also an indissoluble bond that reflects the bond between Christ and the church. And the very act of making a commitment in the sight of others, reinforces and strengthens the internal bond.

In the same way the sacrament of Reconciliation calls for the external action of confessing one's sins and being reconciled with the church community and the internal action of truly feeling sorry for not being our true and best selves—which is who God wants us to be. It is in the external action that we truly feel the internal effects of being reconciled with God, ourselves, and others.

Your appointment with Christ

Every sacrament is an encounter with Christ. A sacrament is meaning-ful because it echoes what Jesus did. Jesus healed people, and we have the sacrament of Anointing. Jesus fed people, and we have the Eucharist. All the sacraments resonate with the actions of Jesus, and one of the greatest things that Jesus did was forgive sinners. That was a huge part of his ministry. When you go to Reconciliation you are encountering the same Christ who forgave Peter and so many others in the gospels and who welcomed Matthew the tax collector and the other disciples even though they had let him down during his hour of suffering.

Reconciliation is a personal encounter with Jesus who is full of mercy and compassion. There is no greater way to experience God's love than to experience God's forgiveness. Forgiveness is not something people deserve. Forgiveness is a gift, and God keeps forgiving us over and over again. When you genuinely celebrate the sacrament of Reconciliation, you tap into the merciful love of God, and that is the most beautiful thing about it.

Following Jesus:
Be ready for some surprises

By Father Ronald Rolheiser, O.M.I.

How do we imitate Jesus? By looking like him or duplicating his actions? How about praying to make us feel the way he did?

FOLLOWING JESUS is not without its surprises. Here's some fair warning! The philosopher Søren Kierkegaard once said that what Jesus wants is followers, not admirers. He's right. To admire Jesus without trying to change our lives does nothing for Jesus or for us. Yet how exactly does one follow Jesus? Classically we have said that we do this by trying to imitate him. But that posits a further question: How do we imitate Jesus?

A negative example might be useful here: The late 1960s saw the flowering of the "Jesus people" with their rather raw, literal approach to following Jesus. They tried to look like he looked. They put on flowing white robes, grew beards, walked barefoot, and tried, in appearance and dress, to imitate the Jesus that centuries of Western artists painted for us. Obviously this kind of thing is not what discipleship means, not only because we don't know what Jesus looked like (although we do know that he was not the fair-skinned, fair-haired young man of Western art), but, more important, because attempts to mimic Jesus' physical appearance miss the point of discipleship entirely.

More subtle is the attempt to imitate Jesus by trying to copy his actions. The algebra here works this way: Jesus did certain things, so we should do them, too. He taught, healed, consoled the downtrodden, went off into the desert by himself, stayed up all night occasionally and prayed, and visited the homes of sinners. So we should do the same things: We should become teachers, nurses, preachers, counselors, monks, social workers, and nonjudgmental friends to the less-than-pious. In this view, imitation is carrying on the actions of Jesus.

Real imitation

This kind of imitation, however valuable as ministry, still is not quite what is required in terms of real discipleship. In the end, it, too, misses the point because one can be a preacher of the gospel and not really be imitating Jesus, just as one can be a truck driver (not something Jesus did) and be imitating him. True imitation is not a question of trying to look like Jesus, nor of trying to duplicate his actions. What is it?

Perhaps one of the better answers to that question is given by John of the Cross, the great Spanish mystic. In his view, we imitate Jesus when we try to imitate his motivation, when we try to do things for the same reason he did. For him, that is how one "puts on Christ." We enter real discipleship when, like Jesus, we have as our motivation the desire to draw all things into one—into one unity of heart, one family of love.

John of the Cross then offers some advice regarding how this can be done. We should begin, he says, by reading scripture and meditating on the life on Jesus. Then we should pray to Christ and ask him to instill in us his desire, longing, and motivation. In essence, we should pray to Jesus and ask him to make us feel the way he felt while he was on earth.

Unexpected developments

Some surprises await us, however, he points out, if we do this. Initially, when we first begin seriously to pray in this way, we will fill with fervor, good feelings, a passion for goodness, and a warm sense of God's presence. We will feel that we feel like Jesus—and that will be a very good feeling indeed.

However, if we persevere in our prayer and desire to imitate him, things will eventually change, and in a way that we least expect. The warm feelings, fervor, and passion—that snug feeling that we feel like Jesus—will disappear and be replaced by something infinitely less pleasant. We will begin to feel sterile, dispassionate, dry. God's presence will feel neither warm nor steady and we will be left wondering: "What's wrong? How did I lose the way?"

As John of the Cross assures us, however, nothing is wrong. Rather, our prayer has been answered. We prayed to Jesus, asking him to let us feel as he felt, and he granted our request. Exactly. For a large part of his life and ministry, Jesus felt exactly as we are now feeling—dry, sterile, and not buoyed up by any warm feelings of God, even as he remained faithful in that darkness. Strange how it can feel, feeling like Jesus.

God in the dryness

There's a fervor that comes from the wetness of fertility that can make the soul swell with feelings of creativity, warmth, and immortality. God is in that. But there is also an aridity the comes from a deeper place, a heat that threatens to dry out the very marrow of the soul, a dryness that shrinks all swelling, especially pride, and leaves us vulnerable and mortal by bringing the soul to kindling temperature. God is in that dryness no less than in the wetness of fertility because in that painful longing we feel the eros of God and the motivation of Christ. And that is how we follow Jesus.

Be a saint in your own way
FATHER JAMES MARTIN, S.J.

Everyone is a unique creation of God, and the way to sanctity is to be your unique self.

THE MOST IMPORTANT spiritual insight I've learned since entering the Jesuits is that God calls each of us to be who we are. "For me to be a saint means for me to be myself," said Thomas Merton. As a result, holiness consists of being true to the person God created. In other words, being holy means being your true self. And besides the life of Jesus of Nazareth, the best illustration of that can be found in the lives of the saints.

I know many readers might groan (inwardly or outwardly) when they hear that. Because, unfortunately, for many people the lives of the saints are considered overly pious and largely irrelevant legends. It can seem almost impossible to relate to people known primarily as marble statues or stained-glass windows. You look at a statue of, say, Saint Thérèse of Lisieux, the "Little Flower," in her Carmelite habit, holding a bouquet of roses and looking heavenward, and it's not hard to think, "What does *that* have to do with my life?"

But it's important to remember that the saints were human beings, which means that they sinned (frequently), doubted (sometimes), and wondered whether they were doing the right thing (more often than you would think). As anyone does, the saints struggled with casting off the vestiges of their false selves and becoming who God wanted them to be.

As an aside, I'm using the term *saints* in its broadest possible meaning: not simply for those who have been "canonized" by the church (that is, officially declared saints and worthy of public veneration) but also for those holy men and women who may not yet be officially recognized as such. But the use of the term in that way has a distinguished background. Saint Paul, for example, employed the same word to refer to his early Christian companions. "To the saints who are in Ephesus," begins one letter (Eph. 1:1). "To the church of God that is in Corinth," he writes in another, "including all the saints throughout Achaia . . . ." (2 Cor. 1:1).

Live the call to holiness

At some point in their lives, each saint realized that God was calling him or her to be faithful in a particular way. Each saint was placed in a different situation and time. Each had a different personality and dealt with life differently. And each related to God a little differently. Just think of the astonishing variety of saints. And I don't mean simply when they lived, what they did, where they were from, or what languages they spoke. I mean something more basic: who they were and how they lived out their call to holiness.

Some examples: Though both of their lives were rooted and grounded in God, Thomas Merton's approach to life resembled very little that of Saint Aloysius Gonzaga, a young Jesuit who lived in 16th-century Rome. Merton was forever questioning his vow of stability, his place in the monastery, and his vocation as a Trappist, until the end of his life. Aloysius Gonzaga, on the other hand, the scion of a noble family, seemed always to have known precisely what he wanted to do—that is, become a Jesuit—from childhood. At a young age Aloysius had to battle both his father and his brother to convince them to allow him to enter the Jesuit novitiate. Merton only had to battle himself. Merton's vocation seemed always to waver. Aloysius' never did.

Or consider Saint Thérèse of Lisieux, the French Carmelite, and Dorothy Day, the American apostle of social justice and founder of the Catholic Worker movement. Thérèse realized that God had called her to spend life cloistered behind the walls of the convent, while Dorothy Day understood that her invitation was to spend a life on the "outside," working among the poor in big cities. Each grasped that. But both appreciated ways of sanctity that diverged from their own. Thérèse, for instance, admired the Catholic missionaries working in Vietnam. And Dorothy Day admired Thérèse.

Blessed Pope John XXIII meditates on this idea in his book *Journal of a Soul*, the compendium of autobiographical writings that he kept from seminary until almost the time of his death. In January 1907 he wrote that we must incorporate the "substance" of the saints' lives into our own. "I am not Saint Aloysius, nor must I seek holiness in his particular way." None of us, he continued, are meant to be a "dry, bloodless representation of a model, however perfect." Rather, wrote John, we are meant to follow the examples of the saints and apply them to our own lives.

"If Saint Aloysius had been as I am," he concluded, "he would have been holy in a different way."

Holy in a different way

Everyone's true self is a unique creation of God's, and the way to sanctity is to become the unique self that God wishes us to be.

Why would Jesus call a tax collector and a religious zealot, and, among his wider circle of disciples, notorious sinners? One reason may have been that Jesus saw each disciple's ability to contribute something unique to the community. The unity of the church, both then and now, encompasses diver-

sity. As Saint Paul wrote: "Now there are a variety of gifts, but the same Spirit
. . . . To each is given a manifestation of the Spirit for the common good. . . .
For just as the body is one and has many members, and all the members of
the body, though many, are one body, so it is with Christ" (1 Cor. 12:4, 7, 12).

All of us bring something unique to the table, and, through our own
gifts, we each manifest a personal way of holiness that enlivens the larger
community. We help to build up the "Kingdom of God" in ways that others
may not. Mother Teresa catches this insight in her most famous saying: 'You
can do something I cannot do. I can do something you cannot do. Together
let us do something beautiful for God."

This diversity is a natural outgrowth of the role of simple human desire,
whose place in the spiritual life is often overlooked. Put simply, the saints had
different desires, and those desires led them to serve God in different ways.
Such desires affected not only what they did but who they became—their true
selves.

These natural inclinations are ways in which God accomplishes his work
in various places and in a variety of modes. When I was studying theology,
our Jesuit community had a small poster hanging in our living room that
offered this little saying about four great founders of religious orders:

Benardus valles,
Colles Benedictus amavit,
Oppida Franciscus,
Magnas Ignatius urbes.

That is:

Bernard loved the valleys,
Benedict the hills,
Francis the small towns,
and Ignatius the great cities.

Each of these four saints found his home in a place suited to his likes and desires and so was moved to accomplish his own particular task. Their individual desires shaped their vocations. Ignatius Loyola, for example, the founder
of the Jesuits, would probably have felt his ambitious plans stymied in a small
town. And Francis of Assisi, the apostle of the poor, would certainly have
gone crazy trying to run a large religious order from a busy office in Rome!

Desire can lead to God

God awakens our vocations primarily through our desires. A man and a
woman, for example, come together in love out of desire and so discover their

vocation as a married couple. Out of desire a husband and wife create a child and discover their vocation as parents in this way. Desire works in a similar way in the lives of the saints, drawing them to certain types of works, giving rise to special vocations and leading to particular styles of holiness. Henri Nouwen became a priest because he desired it. Thérèse of Lisieux entered the convent because she desired it. Dorothy Day entered the Catholic Church because she desired it. Ultimately, one's deepest desires lead to God and the fulfillment of God's desires for the world.

That insight lies behind one of my favorite passages in *The Seven Storey Mountain*. Shortly after his baptism, Thomas Merton is speaking with his good friend Bob Lax. Merton tells his friend he wants to be a good Catholic. "What you should say," says his friend in reply, "is that you want to be a saint." Merton tells the rest of the story:

"A saint? The thought struck me as a little weird. I said: 'How do you expect me to become a saint?' 'By wanting to,' said Lax, simply. . . . 'All that is necessary to be a saint is to want to be one. Don't you believe God will make you what He created you to be, if you consent to let Him do it? All you have to do is desire it.'"

Following these individual desires and inclinations led each of the saints to a distinctive type of holiness. As Thomas Aquinas, the great 13th-century theologian, said, grace builds on nature. Ignatius Loyola ended a military career in 16th-century Spain to follow God, while Joan of Arc began one in 15th-century France. Dorothy Day founded a newspaper to spread the gospel, while Bernadette Soubirous, the famous visionary of Lourdes, shrank in horror from the idea of her story being publicized in the press. Thomas Aquinas spent his life surrounded by books, while Francis of Assisi told his friars not to own even one lest they become too proud. The multiplicity of desires leads to a multiplicity of paths to God.

Enter into the divine

By Sean Reynolds

At Mass, people frequently start with themselves. What would happen if they started with God?

WERE SOMEONE to tell us, as Catholics, that in the liturgy God becomes present to humanity, most would not disagree. At least, not with the idea. But, in our weekly or daily encounter with the liturgy, we often feel as though we witness nothing so serious.

Indeed, the tepidness of parishioners' response at Mass has become the norm rather than the exception. And such a split between our idea and experience is a symptom of our real sense of a personal disconnect from liturgy. We resign ourselves to the role of spectators, judgers of music and prayer from the altar, who occasionally chime in or pray silently. But, whether we deem the experience moving or dull, we nevertheless overlook the only liturgical action that can make it personal: the action of God.

The question of whether Mass was moving and effective has become concerned with the quality of the priest's homily, the choir's singing, the congregation's gusto. Unfortunately, there will always be parishes with uninspired homilies and wretched singers; the church is too large for greatness to be uniform. Nevertheless, cannot—and should not—the liturgy be internally rich and fulfilling for parishioners even in these places? How can we as Catholics take personal ownership over the quality of our liturgical experience and "make it our own"?

Liturgy is divine

In attempts to make laypeople feel more involved in Mass, parishes multiply the various actions (such as the Presentation of the Gifts) that involve the laity into the ritual. Parishioners and liturgists demand also that the music be made contemporary, relatable, what the youth love. Yet, through these innovations we often experience nothing grander. We may feel as though we are less in the midst of a miracle than amongst our own creative energies, a jam session.

By placing primacy on the entrance of ourselves into the liturgy, we undermine the Mass as a gift from God. As Pope Benedict XVI said, "If the various external actions . . . become the essential in the liturgy, if the liturgy degenerates into general activity, then we have radically misunderstood the 'theo-drama' of the liturgy and lapsed into parody."

The predominance of God's liturgical action is perhaps better conveyed by the Eastern Christian word for the Mass: The Divine Liturgy. Here, the very "catholic" notion (in the West as well as the East) that our form of worship is a gift from God finds full emphasis. It is the received form of liturgy, made concrete in rite, that permits us to receive the Body of Christ.

For this reason, the very action that can personally bring us into the liturgy is, as the pope puts it, "participation in the action of God" in the Eucharistic Prayer. When we pray for God to accept our sacrifice and to incarnate before us, the role of the parishioner is no less than that of the priest. There is no performance, but petition. God makes himself accessible to us so that, through our own earthly materials, we can communicate with him in a personal way. As long as this happens, I can never say a liturgy was "ineffective," no matter the speaker or the cantor.

Receive the Other

As for me, I do look to the Mass as outside of me, and thank God that it is. But the Mass is external, not in that it belongs to the culture of some past, and now irrelevant, generation, but in that it belongs to no one on earth; it is divine. And only when I understand that Mass is not of my own in origin (or the priest's or liturgist's) does it become my own *in reception.*

Indeed, there are few things more personal than receiving a gift from another. And were I truly to accept this gift as Wholly Other—with all the discomfort and incongruity with contemporary culture it brings—I would make a truly religious movement. This, for me, is the difficulty of attending Mass. I must train myself to accept the Wholly Other God, who inexplicably makes himself into flesh for my sake and yours.

Does chastity matter?

By Alice Camille

Our values assist us in making responsible choices, including how to use and not misuse the sexual energy that makes us the vital people we are.

WHEN I WAS A CHAPLAIN at a Catholic college 14 years ago, a young woman came to me greatly concerned about her relationship with her boyfriend. Namely, she felt pressured to further the physical intimacy between them. It wasn't all coming from his direction, she wanted to be clear; the urgency was inside her, too. "My parents trust in me," she lamented. "And I know I owe it to the man I'll marry one day not to do this. But I'm afraid I will."

I felt the weight of this woman's sadness and disappointment in herself. But what also seemed apparent to me was her lack of self-possession. She betrayed the belief that she belonged, first to her parents, and later to a husband who had not yet appeared on the scene. Because of this attitude, she couldn't make a decision about her body, her sexuality and dignity and mystery, with her own best interests at heart.

Chastity's invitation

The problem of self-possession is a big one on the road to sexual maturity. We have to own ourselves before we can have the freedom to share ourselves. It's especially acute for people primed with "boundary issues": those who were physically knocked about or sexually molested as children, as well as those who suffered psychological damage to self-esteem or autonomy along the way. But even if we were favored with parents who respected us and gave us the gift of strong, self-reliant identities, arriving at the goal of mature sexuality—chastity—is not necessarily a walk in the park.

For chastity is the goal for all of us, whether we marry, remain single, or enter religious life. As Dominican Father Timothy Radcliffe notes in his excellent book *What Is the Point of Being a Christian?*, even celibates are not married to almost as many people as married people are. Chastity is therefore a virtue we should all seek to deliberately cultivate. So let's start with a definition: What exactly is chastity?

The *Catechism of the Catholic Church* defines chastity as the successful integration of sexuality within the person (no. 2337). This definition speaks of a much greater achievement than preserving one's virginity for one's spouse or simply remaining celibate altogether, which is how many of us were taught to view this virtue. Chastity comes under the cardinal virtue of temperance, which involves "permeating the appetites of the senses with reason"—using discernment to govern physical instinct. Obviously not every impulse we have to eat, drink, buy, take, or do is a wise one. Our values assist us in making responsible choices in all of these matters, including how to use and not misuse the sexual energy that makes us the vital people we are.

If that sounds too academic for you, how about learning how to dance with your "holy hormones," as Catholic psychologists Sister Fran Ferder and Father John Heagle describe the practice of chastity? Most young adults I've surveyed agree that it's hard for them to put "holiness" and "sex" in the same sentence, but that's precisely what chastity invites us to do.

The body's theology

It's also what the late Pope John Paul II did in his famous lectures on the "theology of the body." In 129 Wednesday audiences, the pope offered a gracious, positive, and expansive understanding of the gift of human sexuality—which, frankly, may not be what you might expect of a pope. And that's unfortunate, because the human body is central to Christian doctrine. Think of it: Creation. Salvation. Incarnation. Crucifixion. Resurrection. Ascension. Assumption. How could you even tell the Christian story without noticing the emphasis on the fate of the body?

Our central sacrament—the Eucharist—too, is body-centered. And in the humblest terms all sacraments are about "birth and death, sex and food, sin and sickness," as Timothy Radcliffe points out. If God is to meet us anywhere, it has to be in the body, which is our only real address. It is here that we reside, here that we live and move and have our being.

At the same time, we have to be careful of false distinctions. "We are not spirits trapped in bags of flesh," Radcliffe notes. We are our bodies as much as we are spirit. Escaping that reality is no more possible, or desirable, than escaping our spiritual natures. God, after all, gave us both: the divine likeness embossed in flesh and blood. So we can't expect to give away our bodies without giving over ourselves in some crucial sense, too. Radcliffe describes sexual intimacy as a sacred hour: "Each says to the other: 'Here is my body for you.' It is a profoundly eucharistic act."

Being life-giving

Approaching our sexuality as eucharistic helps us to appreciate the need to be good stewards of this gift. Sacraments are signs whose physical elements participate in deeper and divine realities. We speak of these as mysteries, and it's not hard to see why John Paul II urged in his "theology of the body" that men and women must become masters of their own mystery in embodying and expressing their sexuality.

Clearly this gift involves much more than engaging in sexual, i.e. genital, acts. Our sexuality is unitive energy. It's communion in the widest possible sense. Sexual energy, as Fran Ferder notes, argues against being alone. It generates within us the search for love, family, community, friendship, and creativity of every sort. It even propels the search for God. This is why saints often described their encounters with the Holy One in the language of ecstasy.

John Heagle reminds us that the biological goal of sexual energy is to generate new life. He adds that if we don't answer the call to generativity literally—in sexual intimacy and procreation—the question doesn't go away: How else will we answer the call to give life? Whoever we are, the longing is urgently felt. Chastity is about answering that call moment to moment with integrity according to our station in life.

From here to chastity

But how do we get from "here" to chastity, if "here" is a history of poor sexual stewardship? I'm well aware that if I were a college chaplain today, I wouldn't be encountering as many students worried or guilty about their first sexual experience. Many young people suspect that when it comes to practicing chastity, that ship has sailed and they weren't on it. Many schools support this impression by passing out birth control and condoms rather than educating for a mature understanding of sexuality involving temperance. One of the most surprising defenders of the role of self-mastery in sexuality comes from the little "big" movie, *Juno*. If you haven't seen it yet, run, don't walk to your Netflix queue and order it.

Juno is a 21st-century teen with the opposite problem of the co-ed whose story I told at the beginning. Juno is entirely self-possessed—as children of divorce often need to be. She therefore thinks of her body as a possession: as her property, not her self. This makes it easy to "hook up" with her best friend to find out what this sex business is all about. The "friends with benefits" arrangement is casual, but not as consequence-free as they anticipated.

What Juno learns is how very much she is her body and cannot separate herself from it. A third party—one with *fingernails*, no less—gets hold of her life and from within begins to teach her the connective power of her sexuality. This unborn child assists Juno in healing the memories of her original broken family, strengthening the bonds within her present one, and creating new possibilities for an adoptive mother. Through these experiences Juno learns to trust in people, however imperfect their love is. Her fierce little note to the adoptive mother becomes a manifesto of hope: "If you're still in, I'm still in."

This life-affirming story serves as a beacon for those of us who suspect we've already betrayed the promise of our sexuality by following society's nod to trivializing sex: as entertainment, as romance, or a mere feeding of a biological hunger. Juno can't recover the day before she entered into sexual awareness, but she doesn't have to crawl into the pigeonhole of "sexually active" to which others invariably consign her. Hers is a chastity gained through fire, and she seems ready to be its wise and tender steward.

The *Juno* approach says to the gift of sexuality, and to family, and to the wider community of love: *If you're still in, I'm still in.* It's a far cry from the just-say-no approach of once-popular moral codes that cast human sexuality in a dark and potentially dangerous light—until a sacrament makes it OK.

The nightly news provides us with all too many examples of politicians, clergy, movie stars, and the rare astronaut who have failed to integrate their sexuality into their otherwise mature, responsible, and capable identities. Those who do not master temperance will never be the masters of their own lives. Those who do embrace chastity, having taken up their lives, will be happily prepared in the right hour to lay them down.

A user's guide on the ways to pray

By Linus Mundy

From formal to informal to spoken to silent, the Catholic faith offers a wealth of prayers and ways to pray.

W E NEED TO PRAY; we want to pray. The *Catechism of the Catholic Church* emphasizes this need by saying that "prayer and Christian life are inseparable" and that "prayer is a vital necessity."

But how shall we pray? Fortunately, Catholic tradition as well as contemporary sources are rich in forms of prayer to make our own. You will see many of these prayer forms presented below. They range from the five basic forms of prayer to the classic prayer traditions and practices given to us by illustrious teachers of the faith, such as Saint Benedict, Saint Francis of Assisi, Saint Ignatius Loyola, the Carmelites, and the Dominicans. There are prayers both communal and private. Spoken and silent. Spontaneous and memorized. Formal and informal. Word-filled and wordless.

The ways to pray are endless. But no matter which prayers or prayer forms you make your own, remember to "ground" your prayer in desire and surrender. These are the real essentials for genuine prayer, says writer and Trappist monk Father Thomas Merton. Here is a user's guide on some ways to pray.

Five basic types of prayer

- **Blessing and adoration,** like the Gloria at Mass. We acknowledge God's greatness and power—and mercy—in saving us from evil.
- **Prayers of petition.** Prayer for any need we have (especially forgiveness) but also praying that God's kingdom come and God's will (not necessarily ours) be done.
- **Intercession.** Asking on behalf of another or oneself that God will show mercy and favor.
- **Thanksgiving.** Words/thoughts of gratitude for all things or anything—in the spirit of joy that Christ has set creation free.
- **Praise.** Giving glory to God, recognizing God is God, testifying we are God's children.

Formal, familiar, and often memorized

- **Sign of the Cross.** A mini-prayer acknowledging the Triune God; often an introduction or conclusion to prayer.
- **The Rosary.** Using a string of beads, a form of devotion to Mary consisting of Hail Marys, Our Fathers, and a doxology, all repeated as a meditation.
- **Our Father.** The Lord's Prayer—"the prayer Jesus taught us."
- **Act of contrition.** Formal or spontaneous prayer seeking forgiveness of sins.
- **Meal prayers.** "Grace" before and after meals. Giving thanks. May be formal or informal.
- **Aspirations.** Words/phrases used spontaneously throughout the day to invoke God's help or proclaim God's glory: "Lord, help me"; "God be praised"; "My Jesus, mercy"; and others.

Liturgical, "official" prayers and practices

- **Liturgy of the Hours.** "The official prayer of the church" consists of five parts and is prayed throughout the day: Morning Prayer and Evening Prayer, made up of psalms, canticles, readings; Midday Prayer; Night Prayer; and the Office of Readings complete the Liturgy of the Hours.
- **The Mass.** The "source and summit" of Catholic faith and practice. Also known as the Eucharist; the sacrament commemorating the Last Supper. The Liturgy of the Word is rich in prayers and readily promotes meditation.
- **Prayers at/from the Mass.** Occasions and moments during worship at Mass when formal and informal prayer may rise from the heart; also the common recitation of the Gloria, the Our Father, and other prayers at Mass.
- **Benediction.** Dating to the 13th century, the practice of singing hymns and praises before the Blessed Sacrament.
- **Prayers of Adoration.** Somewhat of a more private and less formalized devotion; kneeling in meditation and worship before the Body of Christ exposed in the form of a consecrated host.
- **Hymns.** Any of an innumerable list of religious songs, usually sung in communion with others, giving glory to God.

Classic, monastic approaches

- **Benedictine.** Daily prayer based on liturgical prayer: psalms, hymns, scripture, and short readings. A specific Benedictine prayer model is *lectio divina*: a practical and sometimes mystical way of praying scripture that moves from reading to studying to listening and finally to praying.

• **Franciscan.** It is said that Saint Francis of Assisi "became prayer." He lived his prayer. His *Canticle of the Sun* is an example of prayer drawing on nature: All the wonders of creation are our brothers and sisters in God.

• **Ignatian.** "Intellectual" prayer, assists us in knowing God. Saint Ignatius of Loyola, founder of the Jesuits, developed his *Spiritual Exercises* where one names a desire and meditates for discernment.

• **Carmelite.** Primary prayer forms are solitude and meditation leading to an interior journey of transformation.

• **Dominican.** Spirituality rooted in the good news of our salvation. Principles include study of scriptural truth and using the whole body in prayer.

Popular, much-loved devotions

• **Novenas.** A nine-day private or public devotion to obtain special graces. Frequently a devotion to a particular saint for a particular need.

• **Litanies.** A sequence or list of petitions followed by responses praying for God's aid. Its repetitive nature emphasizes one's earnestness.

• **The Angelus.** Name taken from the words *Angelus Domini* (the "Angel of the Lord"). A short practice of devotion (notably the Hail Mary) repeated three times each day—morning, noon, and evening—at the sound of a bell.

• **Morning offering.** A prayer for personal holiness, meant to be said upon rising. One offers up everything—one's "prayers, works, joys, and sufferings" of the day ahead for the glory of God.

• **Stations of the Cross.** A series of prayers or meditations at 14 pictures or sculptures depicting the chief scenes of Christ's suffering and death. An ideal Lenten devotion.

Scripture-based prayer

• **God's Word and your prayer.** Selecting specific readings that speak to individual needs, e.g., healing, wisdom, or peace. Read aloud or in silence, listening and meditating on what is read.

- **The Old Testament.** Hebrew scripture, the "prayer book" Jesus and most New Testament writers used, is filled with citations remembering God's covenant with God's people. A wealth of inspiring prayer topics as well as actual prayers.
- **The Psalms.** The complete range of human emotion and need are found in the 150 Psalms of Hebrew scripture. A rich source of "conversation" with God.
- *Lectio divina* (see also the "Benedictine" method). A sequence of: 1. Bible reading; 2. Silence; 3. Meditation on a word or image; 4. Prayer or song rejoicing in God's Word.
- **Canticles.** Songs of prayer. The Magnificat of Mary, in Luke 1; the *Benedictus*, also in Luke 1; and the *Nunc Dimittis*, in Luke 2 are inspiring examples.

Contemplative prayer

- **Meditation.** Taking time to be alone with the One who loves us. An inner prayer that focuses us on the Lord. A "gaze of faith, fixed on Jesus," a "silent love" *(Catechism of the Catholic Church).*
- **Centering prayer.** With emphasis on interior silence, one chooses a sacred word to sustain one's intention to be in God's presence, returning to it as the mind wanders.
- **Walking meditation.** "Prayer-walking" as one consciously, mindfully repeats a word or phrase, putting footsteps and breathing into the same rhythm.
- **The Jesus Prayer** (Prayer of the Heart). From the Eastern Orthodox Church tradition but widely adopted elsewhere. One repeats: "Lord Jesus, Son of God, have mercy on me, a sinner."
- **Christian meditation.** Using a "mantra" (usually *ma-ra-na-tha*—a New Testament word for "Come, Lord Jesus") spoken not only to be attentive but to empty oneself to let in God's Spirit.

Full of grace: Reclaiming the Rosary

BY ALICE CAMILLE

Praying the mysteries of the Rosary we weave our intentions, thoughts, imagination, emotions, and desire for union with Christ.

THE ROSARY HAS EXPERIENCED a recent resurgence in popularity. From kitsch to cool to contemplative tool again, in a single generation—not bad for a devotion that's been kicking around the church in various forms for almost a millennium.

Catholicism was "Marian" a generation ago—or at least, the church gave Protestants plenty of reasons to see it that way. While other Christians adhered to Jesus and the Bible, Catholics prayed to Mary and the saints. That was a false dichotomy, of course, based mostly on externals: Some older Catholic churches were miniature museums of sacred art, with varying degrees of good taste on display. Thoughtful Catholics always understood that they didn't worship Mary, because worship is reserved to God alone. It is *veneration* of Mary that honors her crucial role in the story of Jesus and the life of the church.

"Call your Mother!"

When the Second Vatican Council swept the halls of Catholicism with broad reforms in the late 1960s, the way Catholics expressed their identity on the street changed, too. The church was moving toward a deepened engagement with the modern world. Catholics were all invited to move with it, surrendering a bit of the otherworldly focus that made them seem separate and their witness perhaps too hidden.

For some that movement into the marketplace made scripture and social justice teaching of more practical use than Rosaries and statues. When Catholics turned their attention to the modern world in teaching and testimony, many left relics of the otherworldly—the incense and devotions—behind.

In driving terms, that's called an overcorrection. And it often lands you in a ditch. It rarely helps to replace one dichotomy with another. Minimizing Mary's role in Catholic identity devalues the critical human response to God's initiative that she embodies so beautifully. At the same time, to correct maximizing Mary to the diminishment of Jesus it was perhaps necessary to move a few statues from the center of our worship space, not to mention our mental space. Yet renewed interest in traditional prayer forms today makes the Rosary T-shirt logo sound like wisdom: "Call your Mother. She hasn't heard from you in decades."

Reclaiming the Rosary goes hand in hand with a restoration of Mary's rightful role in Catholic consciousness. What we say about Mary is also necessarily a statement about the church. She is what we must become. Mary models our Christian vocation and shows us how discipleship is done. All teaching about Mary relates to her primary relationship to Jesus. Or as a priest I know likes to say, "We'd never have heard of Mary at all if her son hadn't turned out so well."

Our veneration of Mary is not a cult of personality. She's not a celestial celebrity; she's better than that: She's the one who assures us that saying yes to God, fully and completely, is possible.

Pray, reflect, repeat

So how does the Rosary assist us in becoming more like Mary, that is, "full of grace"? It offers a unique view of the Christian story through the heart of the woman from Nazareth. Mary was the first to ponder the greatest events of salvation history. Through Mary's eyes we reflect on these moments of joy, light, sorrow, and glory and can appreciate the rhythms of life in their sacred dimensions. Birth and death, joy and grief, expectation and loss are not only details of our humanity but mysteries connected to sin and grace. We get to reclaim all the hours of our experience as holy hours when we pass these simple beads through our hands.

One objection onlookers have to the Rosary is that it appears to be a magical device. Although a Rosary may be blessed, Catholics attribute no magical power to its beads. The repetitions of prayers may sound like an incantation, but repetition is a feature, not a formula. So why do we say the same prayers over and over? Does saying something 10 times, or 50 times, make it more sincere?

Ask Saint Peter, who after the resurrection was asked three times: "Simon, son of John, do you love me?" (John 21:15-17). Peter needed to repeat his answer more than Jesus needed to hear it—he'd recently denied his friend and teacher that same number of times. If you're quite sure you haven't turned from grace 50 times, I'm sure one Hail Mary will suffice. Many of us would more likely go another time around those beads.

Repetition is also liberating: It frees the mind to widen into the unconscious. Don't you often think better when you're doing some task you know by heart? Apart from the mechanics of it the Rosary offers us a multiplication of ways to pray. It's scripture meditation, petition, song of praise, and instruction on the faith all at once. Pope Pius XII called it a "compendium of the entire gospel," tracing beliefs about the Incarnation, Epiphany, kingdom of God, Eucharist, Passion, Crucifixion, and Resurrection in jewel-like cameos. Cardinal John Henry Newman declared that the Rosary provides us with a way of "holding in our hands all that we believe"—and it's a whole lot easier to put a Rosary in your pocket than, say, the *Catechism of the Catholic Church*!

The most-repeated prayer of the Rosary is the Hail Mary, which is part scripture—*Hail Mary, full of grace! The Lord is with thee. Blessed art thou among women, and blessed is the fruit of thy womb* (Luke 1:28, 42)—and part supplication—*Holy Mary, Mother of God, pray for us sinners, now and at the hour of our death.* Pope Paul VI emphasized how the Hail Mary hinges on the fatefully placed name of Jesus at its center of gravity. He compared the Rosary to weaving cloth on a loom, identifying the Hail Mary as the warp upon which the mysteries of our faith are woven.

Along with these mysteries we also weave our intentions, thoughts, imagination, emotions, and desire for union with Christ. That's a tall order, which is why the Rosary benefits from a lingering pace. Silence and vocal prayer are its alternating energies. If we race through it, we miss the graced encounter that lurks between the beads. When teaching scripture, rabbis have noted, God speaks in the white space around each letter as much as in the words themselves. White space, or silence, is often where God offers a fresh response to our prayer.

The test of time

Perhaps the most convincing evidence of the Rosary's success is its longevity in practice. In the Middle Ages, a *rosarium* was the term for a collection of devotional readings, but praying on knotted strings had been a poor person's devotion 300 years earlier. At a time when few were literate but many wanted to share in the prayer of the monasteries that loomed above town, reciting 150 *paternosters* (Our Fathers) was as good as chanting 150 psalms as the monks did.

Starting in the 13th century, religious orders such as the Franciscans, Servites, Cistercians, and Dominicans promoted and expanded the Rosary. Its form remained fairly constant until the 20th century, when Father George Preca of Malta, recently canonized, offered a new set of mysteries on the public ministry of Jesus, including the Beatitudes. Admiring the innovation, Pope John Paul II chose to focus on five moments of "epiphany" in which Jesus revealed his divine origins and added the Proclamation of the Kingdom to Preca's reflections to create the Luminous Mysteries.

The Rosary's thoughtful and deliberate history demonstrates that this practice is hardly a theological sideshow in the life of the church. It incorporates the highlights of Christian scripture, doctrine, and liturgy in an entirely accessible prayer form that the humblest person can learn. Even a Doctor of the church can benefit from its wisdom, as Saint Teresa of Ávila did. Toward the end of her life, after the great revelations and ecstasies abandoned her, she focused on the spiritual benefits of one simple prayer: the Hail Mary.

A prayer for everyone

Pope John Paul II suggested that the Rosary, while composed of simple parts, is hardly simplistic. Contained in each drama of its decades is a contradiction: The joy of finding a child also implies the terror of losing one. Presenting a child to God means also surrendering him to his destiny. Christian joy, the pope wrote, is not uncomplicated nor does it imply freedom from care. Adopting the practice of the Rosary prepares us for Christian life as a whole, in which mysteries of joy, light, sorrow, and glory often exchange places in short order.

The Rosary is a traditional prayer, yet its evolution suggests that it also contains much room to breathe in modern times. It can be prayed alone or with others. It is appropriate as family prayer, in preparation for Mass, or to console mourners at a wake service.

Pope John Paul recommended it as a prayer for peace, based on the mystery of Christ who is our peace. A "Rosary personality," he suggested, is a witness against violence, injustice, arrogance, and intolerance in any form. "In turning our eyes to Jesus and Mary, we might regain the ability to look one another in the eye," the pope said (*Rosarium Virginis Mariae,* 41). In which case, praying the Rosary isn't only what traditional Catholics do. It's what all Catholics might want to do more.

Consider Paul, our brother

By Father Donald Senior, C.P.

An apostle and the first great Christian missionary, Saint Paul experienced both conversion and struggle and got some help along the way before finding his vocation.

PERHAPS MORE THAN any other figure in the early church, Paul embodied profound conversion and transformation for the sake of the gospel, both on a personal level and within the religious tradition to which he was passionately committed.

Did the young Paul, immersed in love of his Jewish piety and schooled in the classic literature of Greece, ever imagine some dreamy afternoon in Tarsus that he would travel nearly 10,000 miles—most of it on foot and a lot of it on the sea that he feared—for the sake of a crucified Galilean whom he would come to believe was the embodiment of the divine presence on earth and the revelation of God's love for the world?

Could he ever have imagined that his life story would take him to the imperial city of Rome, as the Acts of the Apostles tells us—not as a curious citizen but bound in a prison ship and held in house arrest in the great city where, nevertheless, he would preach the gospel of Jesus Christ with assurance and without hindrance?

Paul experiences conversion

The New Testament gives us two pictures of a crucial turning point in Paul's life where his vocation from God would burst into flame.

One is found in the dramatic conversion stories of the Acts of the Apostles. Paul, whose zeal drove him to persecute the followers of Jesus, who had watched with approval the stoning of Saint Stephen, who had kept guard over the cloaks of the very men who threw the deadly stones—that zealous Paul would be knocked to the ground by the power of Christ's redeeming presence.

Blinded by the light of God's forgiving love, Paul, paradoxically, would begin to see the truth for the first time. In Luke's account of the unfolding history of the early community, Paul the tormentor and persecutor of the

Christians would now become the "chosen vessel"—the one who would bring the gospel of Jesus from Judea to Antioch and westward to Greece and ultimately to Rome.

Paul's conversion is, in a certain sense, forced from the outside. Incredible experiences beyond his control turn his religious world upside-down and transform his life forever. Only with the help of other Christians was Paul able to make sense of the experiences that had crowded so forcefully into his life that he could no longer see his way. The man who had been so sure in his convictions now is blind and unsure.

His traveling companions on the way to Damascus take him by the hand and lead him to a wise person and a disciple of Jesus, Ananias. Ananias is very nervous about Paul because of his reputation (a background check was undoubtedly needed!) yet comes at the bidding of the Spirit and lays hands on Paul and heals him and helps him understand that indeed God had chosen him to be the instrument that would bring the gospel of life to the Gentiles.

Paul is called

This striking story in Acts about Paul's conversion and call takes a very different form in Paul's own words in the Letter to the Galatians. Reflecting many years later on this life-changing conversion, Paul in his own words presents a different, if complementary portrayal.

There is little mention of dramatic events on the road to Damascus. Looking back, Paul now sees that God had been calling him to this extraordinary transformation from all time. In Galatians, where he reflects on his vocation, Paul cites the great prophetic words of Isaiah 49 and Jeremiah 1: "Now the Word of the Lord came to me, saying, 'Before I formed you in the womb I knew you, and before you were born I consecrated you; I appointed you a prophet to the nations' " (Jeremiah 1:4-5).

Thus, Paul steps into a beautiful and profound biblical tradition—that of the call. That tradition includes Moses at the burning bush, hesitant and tongue-tied; Amos, the herder of sheep and dresser of sycamores, never thinking of himself as called to anything religious; Isaiah struck mute by a sense of his own sinfulness, having his lips purified by a burning coal in a temple vision.

There is Hosea, crushed by the failure of his marriage, drawing from his own suffering an insight into God's enduring love for him and his people; Jeremiah hesitant and fearful, too young for this sort of thing, called by a God who would never abandon him; Mary of Nazareth, still a young woman challenged to a calling beyond imagination.

All of us, I think, can reflect on these different but authentic dimensions of our life. On one level, we are driven by factors outside of us: world events, the economy, the changing face of the church, the movements of culture and history, the encouragement of friends and mentors. And we surely need wise and caring people to help us sort through such experiences and to make sense of them. Like Paul, we need people to help us shed our blindness and see our life and the people around us from the perspective of our Christian faith.

Driven to proclaim the gospel

We can learn something else from our brother Paul. Paul channeled all of his life force into the fulfillment of his God-given mission. This is one of the intriguing mysteries of Paul's life. From the very first moment of his encounter with the risen Christ and the beauty of the gospel message, Paul felt called by God to proclaim this good news not only to his fellow Jews but to the Gentile world.

Even though Paul testifies that he was called to be a missionary to the Gentiles from the first moment he encountered the Risen Christ, still no doubt it took time and the assistance of others for Paul to further develop his initial vocation. By his own testimony he spent considerable time in prayer and solitude in Syria, near Damascus, and then went for a brief time to Jerusalem to confer with Peter and James.

Afterward, he went to Cilicia (his home region in southern Asia Minor) and eventually to Antioch, which would be his first true missionary base. Paul was drafted by Barnabas and brought to Antioch to join him in the new adventure of proclaiming the gospel to the Mediterranean world that lay beyond the perimeters of Israel.

Paul's intense commitment

Paul was not an original or charter member of Jesus' disciples; he was not even a Matthias, chosen late but still one of those who had walked with Jesus from the beginning, as Luke puts it in the early chapters of the Acts of the Apostles. Paul never forgot his second-generation status or, even worse, his wrong-headed persecution of the Christian movement.

He would forever remain in his own estimation as one "born out of due time." But it is equally clear that the sustaining fire of Paul's passion came from the intensity of his commitment to Christ and the good news of God. At one point in his life Paul makes to his community the startling confession: "Christ lives in me."

Paul's ideas—his preaching, his writing, his theology, his teaching—were welded to his own passionate discipleship. He derived his vision from the living soul of the church and his own passionate commitment to it. He was the recipient and responsible guardian of tradition: "I hand on to you what I first received."

Suffering apostle and man of hope

Allow me to cite one final characteristic of Paul. I am convinced from reading Paul's letters that he was a man who suffered greatly from his ministry though it was the consuming passion of his life.

The passage at the beginning of Romans 9 is one of the most poignant, incredible autobiographical passages ever: "I am speaking the truth in Christ, I am not lying; my conscience bears witness in the Holy Spirit, that I have great sorrow and unceasing anguish in my heart. For I could wish that I myself were accursed and cut off from Christ for the sake of my brethren, my kin by race. They are Israelites and to them belong the sonship, the glory, the covenants, the promises; to them belong the patriarchs, and of their race, according to the flesh is the Christ. God, who is over all, be blessed forever. Amen."

Willing "to be cut off from Christ for the sake of his kinspeople"—can we imagine the anguish that wrung that offer from his heart?

At the same time, Paul managed to hold tightly to his hope. I love the passage in Romans 8 where Paul the cosmic doctor seems to ease onto the examination table the body of humanity, this groaning mass of creation. As he reviews the drama of salvation, Paul puts his ear to the heaving chest of the world and decides that the moans and groans he hears coming from the children of God, and even from creation itself, are not death pangs but birth pains—the moans and groans of the Spirit leading all of the created world to God.

Paul never let go of his foundational experience of faith: The love of the crucified Christ for him was the pledge of God's unbreakable covenant, of God's unceasing redemptive love for the world: "Can anything separate us from the love of God?"

"Nothing," he says in the most soaring passage of his letters, "nothing, neither death, nor life, nor angels, nor principalities, nor things present, nor things to come, nor powers, nor height, nor depth, nor anything else in all creation will be able to separate us from the love of God in Christ Jesus" (Romans 8:38-39).

Paul's enduring legacy

In the church of Rome, we know that two apostles are to be remembered. Both Paul and Peter ministered to that church; both died there in testimony to their faith; and the memories of both have formed our church's spirit. Peter's ministry was one of reconciliation and unity. Working from the vantage point of the Jewish Christian community of Jerusalem, Peter exercised his mission in keeping the pieces of the burgeoning community together. Paul, on the other hand, injected into that church a restive spirit of mission and a passion for bold ideas, the apostle of dramatic change and God's new possibilities. He was a champion for the freedom of God's great, world-embracing Spirit.

It is truly an incredible time, an auspicious time, for anyone who seeks to live a profound Christian life in our culture—but how much more so for those who aspire to be ministers of the gospel in the pattern of the Crucified Christ, from whose selfless death came abundant life for the world.

Called to follow Christ

By John W. Martens

What's the purpose of the church, and does it change with the times?

A T THE HEART of the church is *vocation*. The earliest idea of what is today called "church" starts with the Greek word *ekklesia*, which is only found twice in the gospels, both times in Matthew, and means *those who have been "called out."* Jesus "calls out" all who follow him to share in his ministry in different ways.

Before Jesus even preached, healed someone, or performed a miracle, he called people to follow him. At the beginning of Jesus' ministry, after his baptism and temptation in the wilderness, the first thing he did was to call two sets of brothers. He asks Simon and Andrew and then James and John to follow him (Mark 1:16-20). And that is the church in its simplest terms: the followers of Jesus Christ.

Jesus came proclaiming the kingdom, or reign, of God, and it was essential that people responded to that call for the sake of salvation. Even more, though, Jesus chose people to share in his ministry so that the message could be brought more widely, that is, to everyone. Twelve apostles were "appointed," called "to be with him," and "sent out to proclaim the message" (Mark 3:13-19). Jesus sent "them out two by two," instructing them to proclaim "that all should repent" (Mark 6:7-13).

The same, and changing

The church's growth and change allows it to become what it is intended to be: the Body of Christ that is to serve the needs of those both inside and outside the church. The church continues to develop throughout history so that it can fulfill its mission to bring the gospel to the world.

While the mission of the church—the calling and gathering of people as followers of Jesus Christ for the purpose of salvation—is the same as it was when Jesus first proclaimed the gospel and chose the apostles, soon after this early date things in the church began to change. Already in the Acts of the Apostles people were being called specifically to serve Greek-speaking Christians (Acts 6:1-6), and in the second century Ignatius, the bishop of Antioch, spoke of the positions of bishop, priest, and deacon necessary to serve the needs of the growing Christian church.

"There is a growth in the understanding of the realities and the words which have been handed down," says the Second Vatican Council's *Dogmatic Constitution on Divine Revelation* (*Dei Verbum*, no. 8). Sometimes that's because the church needs to refocus on its central mission; sometimes it's because the culture has changed, making the means by which the church has expressed itself less relevant for the current day; and sometimes it might mean that the church is encountering a new culture and finding the best ways to proclaim the gospel in a fresh context. The church must meet and speak to people where they are, and what the church stresses will depend upon the people or culture in which it finds itself. Some examples:

• The internet is a global culture, which requires the presence of the gospel if all peoples are to encounter Jesus. How should the successors of the apostles evangelize online?

• The Western world is less focused on titles and authority than it used to be. So the question today is how should the church bring its message to people less interested in the institutional church and suspicious of institutions in general?

• How does one speak to many people today who are less convinced of the need for God and other fundamental beliefs of the church?

• Pope Francis is not altering the mission of the church in his writing or preaching, but he is emphasizing different aspects of the gospel message and challenging the church to rediscover and reinvigorate itself.

Followers of Jesus

Christians are still calling people to come to the church, God's gathered people here on earth, in order to enter into a relationship with Jesus Christ and prepare for eternal life in the reign or kingdom of God. It is a task that requires new approaches to answer the ancient and eternal call, "Follow me."

Pilgrimage:
The adventure of walking with God

By Pat Morrison

Wherever they may be heading, pilgrims go on a journey of solitude and companionship, silence and prayer, which leads them more deeply into their relationship with God.

FATHER JACK PODSIADLO was already second-guessing his decision big time. Only a few days into what would become his 38-day trek, his feet were blistered, his nose was sunburned, his calf muscles ached—and his "quick-dry" shirt was still wet, so he pinned it to his backpack where it flapped in the breeze like an inelegant flag.

"Walk 500 miles? No way!" was the first reaction of this American Jesuit priest when someone suggested that he walk El Camino de Santiago de Compostela—the Way of St. James of Compostela to the shrine to St. James the Greater in Spain's northwest region of Galicia. The historic *camino*, the challenging trek of hundreds of miles that pilgrims walk (or sometimes bike-ride) for weeks or months, depending on their starting point, usually begins in France or Portugal and ends at the saint's shrine.

Make discoveries along the way

Like thousands of pilgrims before him, Podsiadlo made many discoveries along the way—about himself, about God, about needs real and perceived, and about the values of community and hospitality.

"My inclination to be in charge was [constantly] challenged . . . and the I-am-not-in-control lesson was repeated many times on my way to Compostela," he writes in a story about his pilgrimage in *Company* magazine. "I couldn't always satisfy my email addiction," he writes—nor always get the lower bunk in the pilgrim hostels, or *albergues*, where travelers spent the night.

Pilgrimage also means traveling lightly—and more lightly as time goes on. Podsiadlo had to fit into his backpack everything needed, trying not to exceed one-tenth of his body weight. "Mine was overweight because of the books

I thought I couldn't do without. After a few days I mailed them home . . . ."

Pilgrimage involves only the essentials. For Podsiadlo, that was two sets of underwear, two pairs of pants, two shirts, four pairs of socks, good walking boots, rain gear, and flip-flops.

He also discovered the value of a lightweight sleeping bag because the *albergues* offer bunks or cots but no bedding. "The sleeping bag also served as my sacred space, my only escape from weary, snoring fellow pilgrims."

The *camino* pilgrims had to rely on the kindness of those they met along the way for meals and a kitchen, a hot shower, a place to wash clothes, and toilet facilities. They also learned the value of companionship as they met other pilgrims and walked together for part of the journey, and they got to know their fellow pilgrims in conversation over simple meals and in shared prayer.

Take only the bare essentials

Although his destination was exotic by some standards—not everyone can take a month off to walk across the Spanish Pyrenees—Podsiadlo's *camino* is a typical template for a pilgrimage. Pilgrimage is not jet-set, luxury travel (even though accommodations may sometimes be quite nice and comfortable). There's an inbuilt spiritual discipline that lets spirit connect with the rhythm of walking, hunger, and thirst on the journey to feed one's soul and with a healthy mix of solitude and companionship along the way.

Pilgrimage includes sweat and heat and cold and wind and rain and limited food and food choices. But most pilgrims will tell you those are essential elements to the richness of the experience and the grace of the journey.

Sister Jennifer Mechtild Horner, a Benedictine sister from Beech Grove, Ind., has frequently led college students on pilgrimages. A recent one was to the ecumenical community in Taizé, France.

In her online book *Keep Walking: An Invitation to Pilgrimage*, she describes the student pilgrims' experience, similar to Podsiadlo's, of lugging too much "stuff" and consequently getting weighed down by it—a physical reminder of a deeper spiritual reality.

She also shares her own realization about her relationship with food as she stood in a long line waiting for what looked like a way-too-small portion to be doled out. "As I got to the front of the line [filled with a couple thousand people] and had my supper portioned out for me . . . it all hit me full force. . . . Looking at the roll and rice dish on my plate and the sweet tea in my bowl, I went into frightened mode. How would I handle this? There was the temptation to try to get more and save it for later. . . . But as I allowed myself to receive what I was given, I realized that I had enough. . . . One of the things I learned at Taizé was that there is abundance in having enough and nothing more. I will carry this insight with me for the rest of my life as a gift."

A way to pray with body and soul

According to Webster's, a pilgrimage is: 1. a journey to a shrine or sacred place, or 2. a long journey or search, especially one of an exalted purpose or moral significance.

For all religious travelers, pilgrimage is an outer journey that mirrors, even in some unconscious way, a quest for interior development or transformation. This innate desire to connect with the holy in specific geographical spaces is more than mere tourism.

Pilgrimage is part of devotional practice, whether suggested or required, for most of the world's great religions. For Jews, the pilgrimage to Jerusalem and its Temple has been a treasured part of their faith from biblical times. A once-in-a-lifetime pilgrimage to Mecca for every Muslim who can undertake it is one of the Five Pillars of Islam, together with the profession of faith, daily prayer, fasting, and almsgiving. Buddhism and Hinduism also encourage pilgrimages to holy sites.

For the three Abrahamic faiths—Judaism, Christianity, and Islam—the lands of the Bible and Qur'an, especially Jerusalem, are indeed the "Holy Land." For Christians, the places associated with the life, death, and resurrection of Jesus hold special prominence. Besides Jerusalem, these include Bethlehem, Nazareth, the sites linked to John's (and Jesus' own) baptism, and the many towns and villages where the gospels say Jesus ministered, healed, and taught.

Pilgrims everywhere

As we've seen, pilgrimage is not limited to the Holy Land. Especially in the Roman Catholic tradition, the global landscape is rich in places frequented for centuries by God-seekers. And a pilgrimage can be as simple as a good, long hike coupled with prayer.

For the past eight years on the Saturday before Mother's Day, rain or shine, a pilgrimage has taken place in central Ohio to pray for church vocations. Organized by the Sisters and Missionaries of the Precious Blood and the Archdiocese of Cincinnati, pilgrims of all ages take the approximately eight-mile "Stepping Up the Call: Lifting Soles and Souls for Vocations" walk or ride to an average of six churches and holy places in Mercer and Auglaize counties. There's time for prayer, song, fellowship, and healthy snacks, and the pilgrimage always includes the Rosary and eucharistic adoration.

"Stepping Up the Call" has become a popular annual event that's grown each year—in 2011 more than 200 people participated from across Ohio and Indiana. Young families with babies in strollers, adult children pushing a praying parent in a wheelchair, and song and prayer along the way make it a microcosm of the church.

Whether it's on the road to Compostela, under a tent in Taizé, praying in the grotto of Lourdes, or walking the highways of central Ohio, a pilgrimage can be a transforming, graced time like no other—a walk with the God who always calls us more deeply into the mystery of God's love.

What do Catholics mean by "authority"?

By Alice Camille

When it comes to the big issues in life, you want to find the source that speaks with integrity and can point you in the right direction. That's what the teaching office of the church is for.

I KNOW SOME THINGS, and so do you. No one lives very long in this world without picking up a certain amount of experience, knowledge, and wisdom on-the-go. But I'll be the first to admit that not everything I *think* I know is really so. Not every idea I carry around in my head (and on which I bet my daily decisions) is dropped in there by cosmic revelation. Angels rarely talk to me—or if they do, I don't always listen up.

But what do we do when we're not sure that the information we're working with is accurate? In the information age, the answer's obvious: Troll for the facts. A Google search has provided a one-stop solution to simple problems I've recently had, such as determining how to cook a still-frozen turkey; where to buy waterproof boots; figuring out how many movies Patrick Swayze made. But as we all learn, some sources for "the facts" are more reliable than others.

We learn, in other words, that gathering information isn't enough. Not all resources for the truth are created equal. Some sources are authoritative. Others offer more or less what I'm already doing: caging the odds and making my best guess. That is why we have authority, and why we need it.

A big deposit

In matters of faith, Catholics have developed a structure of authority known as the *magisterium*. It's the teaching power of the church, laid down in gospel terms when Jesus calls Saint Peter his rock and later when the apostles are on hand in the upper room to receive the guiding and illuminating Holy Spirit. Through apostolic succession—the "laying on of hands" that confers leadership on each new generation of the church—connection to that original authority has been protected and passed forward. I know that there's little in my life of faith that doesn't come to me directly or indirectly as a result of 20 centuries of magisterial collaboration.

What does the magisterium provide for each generation of the church? It's entrusted with the deposit of faith: that "trustworthy teaching" scripture refers to that guarantees "a remarkable harmony" between the church's leadership and faithful membership, in the words of the *Catechism of the Catholic Church*. The deposit of faith doesn't belong to the clergy alone, guarded in a hallowed vault of truth, but is the treasure of the whole church. We maintain it by professing and practicing together what has "come to us from the apostles," as we say at Mass.

Pope John Paul II reminded the church that an earlier pope, Pius XII, once declared that "lay believers are in the front line of church life; for them the church is the animating principle of human society. Therefore, they in particular ought to have an ever-clearer consciousness of not only belonging to the church, but of being the church." In fact, we believe that the church's teaching authority is informed and animated by the *sensus fidelium*, or "sense of the faithful": "The faithful have an instinct for the truth of the gospel, which enables them to recognize and endorse authentic Christian doctrine and practice, and to reject what is false" (from the Vatican document *Sensus fidei in the life of the church*, 2014).

How do we express the deposit of faith all together, then, as a church from the bishops to the last faithful disciple? Through thoughtful attention to and study of scripture. By being informed about the long history of doctrine and the documents that make up church teaching, including those being added regularly by local bishops and the pope today. By participating in the sacramental life of the church and nourishing our own spiritual growth. Speaking of faith as a deposit might sound like it's something locked up for safekeeping to prevent it from being stolen or damaged. Actually, nothing could be further from the truth! This is one treasure that needs to get out more.

The deposit of faith comes in two main containers, marked *scripture*, which is no longer added to, and *tradition*, which expands with each new age. Which came first, people often wonder, and which is more important? That is a little like saying: Which came first, your mother or your father? While one may be older by calendar years, neither was technically your parent until they both came together and you were conceived. In the same way, while sacred texts of many kinds were written by prophets and sages for centuries, the book we call the Bible didn't exist until the community of the church compiled, sorted, and confirmed its contents.

The tradition of the church is therefore responsible for scripture as we know it. Yet it's unfair to say tradition came first because it took those ancient writings and so many more to produce the community who would know itself as the People of God. The texts existed, and the community existed, and when the two came together inspired by the Holy Spirit, both scripture and tradition took their first unified breath. And then the magisterium, or teaching church, provides and promotes this ever-deepening and increasing deposit of faith. As the catechism puts it: "Sacred Tradition, Sacred Scripture and the Magisterium of the Church are so connected and associated that one of them cannot stand without the others. Working together, each in its own way, under the action of the one Holy Spirit, they all contribute effectively to the salvation of souls."

The papacy:
Five reasons young adults love Pope Francis

By Catherine Loftus

Like his predecessor Pope John Paul II, Pope Francis has a particular appeal to young people around the world with his simple message of compassion and mercy. Here is one young Catholic's list of why the pope has such kid cred.

POPE FRANCIS has everyone talking, but young people especially are loving him! In a changing world, it seems as if the current pope understands that the church must continue evolving even as it ensures that the truth of the gospel is being heard and received. Pope Francis' focus on the love and mercy of Christ and the joy of the gospel is refreshing for the younger generation of Catholics. He brings simplicity to a role that has sometimes been seen as overly ostentatious and rigid in years past.

1. He's all about the people.
Let the little children come to me, and do not stop them; for it is to such as these that the kingdom of heaven belongs (Matthew 19:14).

Pope Francis is known for taking selfies with bystanders, reaching out to children, and building connections with those who gather to see him. This is part of what makes the pope feel approachable to young people. He is willing to take risks and step outside what he calls the "sardine can" of the popemobile to guide the church and make all feel welcome.

2. Who am I to judge?
Do not judge, so that you may not be judged (Matthew 7:1).

These now famous words of Pope Francis resonated strongly with Catholics and non-Catholics everywhere. In a world where divisive political topics often overshadow the big picture of the church, Pope Francis made clear the church's central message of love. This spoke volumes to young people to see the leader of the church making a strong statement that people are more important than politics. These words hinted at changes in the church that many young people want to see.

3. He is transforming the papal office.

Foxes have holes, and birds of the air have nests; but the Son of Man has nowhere to lay his head (Luke 9:58).

From refusing to live in extravagant quarters to choosing modest vestments and cutting bonuses in the Vatican, Pope Francis is the epitome of a humble servant. He is dedicated to the poor and marginalized and is showing the world that the Catholic Church can talk the talk and walk the walk. He is encouraging service and sacrifice not by telling, but by doing. This is a powerful message for young people, and one that is inspiring service around the world.

4. He uses Twitter.

When Jesus had come down from the mountain, great crowds followed him (Matthew 8:1).

And he has more than 12 million followers! Pope Francis was named *Time*'s Person of the Year, and he was on the cover of *Rolling Stone*. He is getting lots of media attention for how he is changing the public face of the church, and this is yet another way he is reaching young people. With his use of social and traditional media, people of all faiths are getting to see how love and acceptance are a part of Catholic teaching. In a world where many young people feel it is taboo to talk about religion, Pope Francis is making it cool.

5. He is human.

He did not regard equality with God as something to be grasped ... being born in human likeness and being found in human form ... (Philippians 2:6b, 7b).

Pope Francis said of himself: "The pope is a man who laughs, cries, sleeps well, and has friends like everyone else; a normal person." It is this humble attitude and the normalcy that he brings to the papal office that has captivated audiences, both young and old. He has spoken time and time again about how he is a regular guy and enjoys things like World Cup soccer and motorcycles. He does not view himself as living above the people he serves, but as one who walks with all of us in our journey to follow Christ. I believe this is the most important part of Pope Francis' ministry. He is out working with people, talking to people, and adapting his role as a world leader and religious leader to communicate with and relate to ordinary people, especially young people, in hopes of bringing the world closer to Christ.

Why Catholics care about people living in poverty

BY SISTER SUSAN ROSE FRANCOIS, C.S.J.P.

Whether it's getting the oatmeal right in a soup kitchen or advocating to end global poverty, Catholics should and do care about those on the margins of society.

W OULD YOU LIKE your toast buttered or dry?" This important question was key to my early-morning ministry to men and women experiencing homelessness on the streets of London, England. I had traveled 3,000 miles across the Atlantic Ocean to live in community with my British Sisters of St. Joseph of Peace during my novitiate ministry experience. Each morning I left the comforts of our house at the crack of dawn in order to have the tea ready and the toaster warmed up when our first clients walked in the door. As I struggled to get out of my warm and toasty bed while it was still dark outside, I would think of the men and women waking up on park benches or, if they were lucky, in an overnight shelter. I may have been preparing to profess a vow of poverty, but these people lived real economic poverty each day.

The Passage Day Centre for the Homeless, a collaborative ministry of London's Westminster Cathedral and the Daughters of Charity of St. Vincent DePaul, provides far more than a hot breakfast to men and women "sleeping rough" on the city's streets. Staff and volunteers help clients find housing, seek employment, gain literacy, and learn computer skills. Counselors and healthcare workers provide mental and physical care. Chaplains offer spiritual care, daily Mass, and common prayer. Combined, these efforts treat the whole person with dignity and empower these men and women to rebuild their lives.

The preferential option

Of course, I did not need to travel 3,000 miles to find people experiencing poverty. Here in the United States, the poverty rate is increasing at an alarming rate. About 45 million Americans live below the poverty line.

The Catholic faith calls us to live out a "preferential option for the poor and vulnerable." What that means in the simplest of terms is that we, as a society, must put the needs of people living in poverty and vulnerable situations first. By *option* the church does not mean "optional" but rather that we need to opt, or choose, to act on behalf of people living in poverty.

Caring for people who are poor has been part of what it means to be a Christian from the very beginning. Since its earliest days, the church has drawn inspiration from Old Testament prophets and none other than Jesus himself in discerning the Christian response to poverty. In the Gospel of Luke, when Jesus began his public ministry, he was handed a scroll of the Prophet Isaiah and read these words aloud in the synagogue: " 'The Spirit of the Lord is upon me, because he has anointed me to bring glad tidings to the poor. He has sent me to proclaim liberty to captives and recovery of sight to the blind, to let the oppressed go free, and to proclaim a year acceptable to the Lord' " (Luke 4:18-19).

As anyone who has read the rest of the story knows, he went on to do just that. Jesus lived in solidarity with, and ministered in loving action to, people who were poor and vulnerable in his own time. As Christians following in his footsteps today, we are called to do the same.

Shoes on the ground

The recent economic crisis has only increased the number of people turning to parishes and nonprofits for help. In the face of such rising poverty, those of us who count ourselves members of a church committed to loving action have our work cut out for us. Perhaps this is why Pope Benedict XVI reminds us that "justice is inseparable from charity, and intrinsic to it" (encyclical letter *Caritas in Veritate*, no. 6). We can think of charity and justice as the "two feet" of Christian discipleship. To follow Jesus, we can't only hop on one foot, either providing charity or acting for justice. We need to do both. Otherwise, we as a society will fall over, while those who are poor and vulnerable will fall into, and through, the cracks.

Charity is *very* important. As the pope writes in his encyclical *Deus Caritas Est*, the "church cannot neglect the service of charity any more than she can neglect the Sacraments and the Word" (no. 22). For one thing, charity is often quite literally a matter of life and death for those in need. If a mother in a drought-stricken region of the world does not receive emergency food assistance, her child might die of starvation. Providing charity is also an essential part of what it means to be a Christian. When we volunteer at a homeless shelter or soup kitchen, we remember the words of Jesus: "Whatever you did for one of these least brothers or sisters of mine, you did for me" (Matthew 25:40).

Doing more

The call to loving action, however, does not stop at charity. Remember the two feet. We must also look closely at the root causes of poverty and seek to change them through actions for justice. For example, let's say you are a regular volunteer at a shelter for pregnant women. In conversation with the women, you learn that many have been approved for government assistance that would help them get into permanent housing, but the waiting list is more than one year long. What can you do? You are already walking with the foot of charity by helping at the shelter. As you step with the other foot, the foot of justice, you might call your elected representatives and share the story of the women. You can advocate for legislative or policy changes to increase access to affordable housing.

As the U.S. Catholic Bishops said in their pastoral letter *Economic Justice For All*, the preferential option for the poor calls us 'to speak for the voiceless" (no.16). Something powerful happens when people come together to speak on behalf of justice. For the past four years, I have joined more than 350 faithful citizens—women religious, clergy, parishioners, and Catholic service and justice organizations—for Catholic Advocacy Day in Washington state. We journey to the state capitol to speak with one voice on behalf of people who are poor and vulnerable.

Global dimensions

Saint Pope John Paul II observed that in these times the preferential option for the poor "has to be expressed in worldwide dimensions, embracing the immense number of the hungry, the needy, the homeless, those without medical care and those without hope" (encyclical letter *Sollicitudo Rei Socialis*, no. 42). Our call to loving action extends beyond our own communities and even our own national borders.

How can you respond to global poverty? Taking a step for charity, you can support the efforts of groups like Catholic Relief Services (CRS), the official international humanitarian agency of the U.S. Catholic community. CRS is on the ground in more than 100 countries serving more than 100 million people in need. Taking a step for justice, you can join Catholics Confronting Global Poverty, an effort of the U.S. Conference of Catholic Bishops and CRS that seeks to mobilize 1 million Catholics to pray and advocate to end global poverty. You can sign up for electronic advocacy alerts on their website, crs. org/globalpoverty.

Human dignity

Ultimately, the call to preferential love for people who are poor and vulnerable stems from the reality that each of us, no matter our economic status, is created in the image and likeness of God. We have inherent human dignity and the right to life. That means we also have a right to those things that are necessary to live a dignified life, including food, shelter, education, employment, health care, and housing.

That became very clear to me as a novice when I ministered at the Passage Day Centre. In addition to my toast duties, I sometimes helped out on the hot breakfast line. One day, I served an elderly woman a large helping of porridge, or as we Americans like to call it, oatmeal. A few moments later she returned, her bowl barely touched. "I'd like to speak to the chef," she declared in a very dignified voice.

I went back into the kitchen and relayed the message. The gentleman who had been cooking that day's breakfast put down his spatula, smoothed out his apron, and walked out to the front counter. They engaged in a lengthy and civilized discussion on the preferred qualities of porridge. Apparently, in her opinion, that day's batch of porridge had been far too runny.

A few hours later, after we closed down our breakfast operation, I went back into the kitchen and spoke to the chef. He thanked me for interrupting his cooking so that he could speak to the woman. "Sometimes they just need an opportunity to speak their truth," he said. "After all, she doesn't have control over much in her life. Listening to her opinion on the quality of our porridge is the least I can do for her." He clearly recognized that she was not merely a homeless woman but a person with inherent dignity. In choosing to listen to her so attentively, he exercised his option for the poor and vulnerable.

Can your body be sacred in the age of twerking?

BY SISTER SUSAN KIDD, C.N.D.

Despite media messages to the contrary, we feel whole and true to ourselves when we care for our bodies.

I AM FORTUNATE ENOUGH to have a steady stream of university students through my office, and I asked them this question: "Can your body be sacred in the age of twerking?" I was not ready for their response: silence, an exchange of glances between them, and then a giggling shy look in my direction.

That was not normal. There is often a buzz of chatter in my office, usually accompanied by laughter and on some days with an equal balance of tears; some conversations have both! I am a campus minister, hired by the Catholic Church to work on a secular university campus. The people through my office vary from day to day and include students, staff, and faculty. This day, this question caused the audience to pause. But it shouldn't have.

We were created to care for creation

I am here to tell you that the answer to the question is a clear and resounding "yes!" Despite the relentless media messages that leave us with the impression that there are no boundaries, protections, or sense of sanctity left when it comes to our bodies, the reality is that we feel whole and true to ourselves when we care for our bodies. That is because we are created in God's image and likeness. We are blessed with duties and responsibilities to be good stewards of all creation, including ourselves—our minds, hearts, *and* bodies.

Our rich Catholic teachings on chastity and integrating the powers of life and love are meant to free us to be our best selves. Being chaste is about being in right relationship with God and ourselves and in healthy relationships with others. But sometimes we focus too much on relationships with others at the expense of our relationship with ourselves and God. The "great commandment" (Matthew 22:37-38)—to love God with all our hearts, souls, and minds—reminds us that focusing on our personal relationship with God above all others is not being selfish. It is being faithful.

Pressured to choose poorly

I believe it is easier for me as a religious sister to live chastely than for those who have not yet made a life choice. I have my public commitment, my congregation, prayer, community, ministry, and the other vows supporting me. Those considering religious life have many external pressures luring them toward options that are not life-giving. But that is not to say that the pressures are insurmountable. We must constantly call ourselves back to our purpose: which is to live in the joy of Christ. It's difficult to see where twerking fits into that plan.

Yet that is not to say that using your body in expressive ways is bad. For example, when some students of different cultures come through my office, they sing and dance with thrusting hips! They are quick to hug and touch. This reflects a healthy sense of sexuality and of self. Embracing, dancing, rhythmic and meditative movement, and exercise can model healthy living. And all are in keeping with our Catholic tradition of celebrating our flesh-and-blood humanity.

Lessons in sanctity

The sanctity of the human body is both caught and taught. We need more occasions to discuss such important topics among peers and family members. In this fast age of social media, it takes but one careless decision to change someone's reputation for a very long time.

Recently with my permission, my students added SnapChat to my phone. Now I receive pictures from them—"clean fun" my mother would call it. But I can see how this technology could be used differently given other people and other choices—sexting and cyber-bullying to name but a few examples. We need to treasure the gift of human sexuality and not denigrate it or ourselves.

Our flesh-and-blood God

It is through God's great act of love that Jesus became human. At the Eucharist we are invited to remember the Incarnation with all of our senses: We take and eat God's Body and Blood. What an intimate sign of union, intimacy, and the inner unity of body and spirit. Jesus is wholly present in us. That's sanctity of the body!

We are the vessels God chose to carry on the message of Incarnation to the ends of the earth. And yet, we carry this message in clay pots (2 Corinthians 4:7). It is up to all of us—from athletes to idols, to teachers, parents, friends, and family—to promote positive body images of men and women and a healthy understanding of our sexuality and sanctity. We can start by treating our bodies and the bodies of others with due respect.

What the parish has to offer

BY FATHER PAUL BOUDREAU

The parish is a spiritual home away from home, a gathering of people called and chosen to represent God in the world.

W HEN I WAS A KID growing up in New England, a Catholic kid, everything I did revolved around the parish. It's where I went to church with my parents and my brother every Sunday and all the holy days. It's where I played sports. I was on the championship basketball team and the bowling team. My brother and I were altar boys, and my mother served on several committees that had to do with parish life. My dad helped out taking care of the grounds around the church, and he belonged to the Knights of Columbus.

I belonged to the Boy Scout troop that met in the church hall. That wasn't expressly Catholic, but because it met in the church, most of the guys in the troop were from the parish. All the kids I hung around with in school belonged to the parish. We were all part of the CYO, the Catholic Youth Organization that kept us active after confirmation. We even skipped CYO meetings together. Granted, when we ditched CYO we often did some very un-Catholic things, but we did them together, and together is what made us a community.

A common mission

The word *parish* comes from the Greek word *paroikia*, the root of our English word "parochial," a combination of *para*, which means "near" or "beside" and *oikos*, which means "house" or "home."

In the Bible, the word paroikia meant sojourning or dwelling in a foreign land, or a "community of sojourners," which referred to the Jewish people when they lived outside of Judea. Later in the Christian era, the term was applied to the earthly life of Christians living in a temporal abode (1 Peter 1:17, 2:11). By the end of the fourth century, the word was used to describe the local Christian community.

I haven't played basketball in a while and I can't remember the last time I went bowling, and I live a couple of thousand miles from where I grew up, but I still call the parish in which I now live my home. I'm always a little shocked when people ask me if I'm "going home" for the holidays. "I am home," I explain to them before I tell them about my plans to visit my family.

The parish for me is a community of like-minded people I find nowhere else. Oh, there's a rich and sometimes disturbing diversity of thought, but the foundation, the root, is the same. No matter how different we might be politically or socially, we all grow from the same belief in who we are, why we're here, and where we're going. Our creed is one.

We share a common mission: to be the Body of Christ. One of the great things about being Catholic is that we're all sacraments, visible signs of the invisible God. To the degree that our lives, our thoughts, words, and deeds, conform to those of Christ, to that degree we make Christ real in the world. We are baptized into Christ, incorporated into his Body. We possess his Spirit. We eat and drink the reality of his presence. His flesh is our flesh; his blood flows in our veins. This mystical communion we have with Christ creates an affinity like no other. The grace of God at work in us knits us together and makes us one. We are the community of God.

Being together

Not that we're perfect by any means. Quite to the contrary. We're very imperfect people. Despite being the People of God, we are a family of sinners. That puts us at odds and in conflict with each other on a regular basis. There are factions in the parish, extremes of thought about what makes and what fails to make people Catholic. Our thoughts, words, and deeds are not uniform. In the community of peace there is discord; the common bond of love is sometimes broken by injury and animosity.

For this illness of spirit, for this breakdown of togetherness, God offers a remedy: forgiveness. It is the glue that keeps the parish united.

The great theologian Saint Thomas Aquinas wrote that the sacraments "effect what they signify." In other words, when Catholics celebrate forgiveness in our parish liturgies, as we do in the sacraments of Eucharist, Reconciliation, and Anointing, forgiveness actually happens. Our faith in "one baptism for the forgiveness of sins" takes effect not only in reconciliation between ourselves and God but also in the parish between ourselves and each other.

God's infinite forgiveness, which we tap into individually or communally in the sacraments, fills our lives to overflowing. It is this superabundance of forgiveness poured out in us that spills over into the lives of others in the parish. We can forgive as we are forgiven, and the bond of love is maintained.

Plus, we have great potluck suppers. It's no coincidence that the central act of our religion is eating and drinking. The Eucharist is the source and summit of our faith. Our full, conscious, and active participation in the celebration of the Eucharist effects the presence of Christ in the parish. And through us, the parish, Christ is experienced in the greater community. It's no wonder, then, that we keep the ball rolling, so to speak, by having many gatherings in which we exercise and enjoy our friendship in Christ.

Potluck suppers are a great way to get together. So are Bible study groups, small faith communities, prayer groups, children's play groups, after-Mass coffee and donuts, parish soup kitchens, organizations like Catholic Daughters of America and Knights of Columbus, which all bring us together to experience this fellowship we have in Christ.

Where the rubber meets the road

We're not called the Roman Catholic Church for nothing. Rome is our center. It's where the pope lives and where the Vatican conducts its work of guiding and administering the universal church. The pope, who is the successor of Saint Peter, appoints bishops, who succeed the apostles, to lead the church locally in the form of dioceses, which encompass large geographical areas. In turn, a diocese is further broken down into parishes, over which the bishop appoints pastors, who are the bishop's representatives. The parish is the smallest administrative division of the church, but it's where the rubber meets the road. Without the parish, the church would be all talk and no action.

Finally, the parish is where vocations to religious life and the ordained ministry are spawned. God's call, like everything God does, comes through the instrumentality of people. Men and women are inspired to offer their lives in service to the church through their experience of the parish. When parish life is good, people like you and me want to dedicate themselves more fully to it. When parish life is not so hot, we want to work full time to make it better. Or maybe we're so inspired by parish life that we want to bring this wonderful and rewarding experience to places and people who have never had the pleasure. Then we become missionaries.

So whether you belong to a parish as tiny as St. Genevieve's that comprises one block of downtown Fresno, Calif., or the huge Archdiocese of the Military Services, U.S.A., a single parish that serves all military personnel and their families throughout the entire world, or to a national parish created to serve a particular language group or immigrant community such as St. Joseph's German Catholic parish in Detroit or Sagrado Corazón de Jesús Spanish parish in Windham, Conn., you have a spiritual home away from home, a community of friends, a gathering of people called and chosen to represent God in the world—to be the living, breathing sign of God's love and compassion for all people. Enjoy.

Why we care about the common good

BY BRYAN FROEHLE

For Catholics, the common good starts with the idea that a good society must have the good of all people and the whole person as its primary goal.

CATHOLIC TEACHING pointedly does not refer to human beings as individuals but rather as persons. An individual is a separate entity, a detached unit, without any necessary relationship with others. A person, however, has a personality, a unique sense of self to which others, including God, the ultimate Other, relate. Seen in this light, the goal of any given human society or organization is to advance the fullness and flourishing of the human person.

The Catholic emphasis on the person and the common good is intimately tied to the teachings of Jesus revealed in scripture and seen with the eyes of faith. In the Catholic tradition, all humanity is potentially heir to the promise of Jesus' death and resurrection, God's giving of God's self for all persons, equally, for all time. The Catholic vision of the common good, then, is ultimately affirmed in the experience of God's love for humanity, of God's saving grace.

Institutional and incarnational

Outsiders and insiders alike often admire Catholicism for its institutions, social vision, and spirituality. These three dimensions are interrelated within Catholicism and all flow from its incarnational, sacramental understanding of the world. This Catholic perspective helps us understand what it means to pursue the common good. Just as Jesus is understood as a loving God incarnate in human flesh, so the institutions that Catholicism has nurtured can be understood as an "en-fleshment" of the healing ministry of Jesus within our particular time and place.

The social vision of Catholicism that creates such institutions is rooted in the accumulated wisdom of 2,000 years of thought about war and peace, the nature of a good society, poverty, and justice. It offers a resource to all of Christianity and humanity in general. The Catholic tradition understands God's grace as something freely given, to all humanity, without reservation. It is from this experience of God's grace that all the various spiritualities found within Catholicism spring.

Discerning the common good

Catholicism is distinguished for its diverse spiritual traditions. Few other religions present such an immense spiritual breadth and depth. These range from a rich diversity of monasteries and retreat centers to distinctive writings of mystics and other holy women and men through the centuries. They include often contrasting spiritual traditions—Benedictine, Ignatian, Dominican, and Franciscan, just to name a few. Each of these traditions offers a variety of tools for discernment, tools that also aid in discerning the common good.

The *Catechism of the Catholic Church* names three dimensions to pay particular attention to in such discernment: tradition, creation, and history (2705), together with a fourth: life (2706). *Tradition* includes scripture (especially the gospels), liturgical, spiritual, and related writings. *Creation* refers to everything about the physical world around us. *History* encompasses what we know of society, past and present, including human culture, psychology, and personality. Finally, *life* is what we, personally, have experienced and how we have come to be shaped by and learn from that experience. The common good is best discerned when we are attentive on all four levels at the same time.

But discerning the common good requires more than simply having tools in hand. One must also have a clear idea as to what is meant by the "common good." That understanding starts with how we understand the nature of the human being.

Right relationship and the common good

The origin of the word *religion* is said to be "religare," to reconnect. Saint Augustine pointed out that such a meaning suggests that religion is about relationship—a particularly appropriate observation for a theologian famous for the remark that our hearts are restless until they rest in God. Religion is about connecting and is even tied to the yearning to fill an emptiness inside ourselves that can only be filled in right relationship.

For this reason, another way to understand the common good is as the sum of all conditions of social life that allow for right relationship. The common good is realized through right relationships that allow for true human flourishing. The common good flows from the unity and equality of all.

To understand how Catholicism envisions this chain of interactive relationships that is Catholicism's understanding of the human experience and humanity's relationship to God, think of the story of the butterfly halfway around the world. As the story goes, the flapping of that one butterfly's wings can interrelate with a whole series of other events, changing experiences on the other side of the world. If this is the case for butterflies, the Catholic tradition would insist, so much more is it the case for humanity and for our collective common good.

Go viral with the gospel!

By Alice Camille

Some practical ways to share your faith with others.

W E KNOW, WE KNOW: We're supposed to share our faith. We're not supposed to cram it under a bushel but take it to the ends of the earth. Evangelization—that big tangle of a word—is basically Greek for going viral with the gospel. But how, precisely, are we supposed to do that without, well, being creepy?

Use words if necessary

The creepy-factor is significant, because every message comes embedded in its medium, and that context lingers. Recently, I was watching an old episode of *The Vampire Diaries*—one of my guilty pleasures. A werewolf character who used to be a villain insisted he was now with the good guys because, frankly, he needed redemption. For Christians, of course, that's a super-loaded word. *Redemption* literally means your ransom's been paid and you've been rescued. You can't redeem yourself: You're dependent on those who love you to make the drop-off. My attention was momentarily diverted to the theological implications of a born-again werewolf, but it was hard to forget that this dude seeking redemption was last seen ripping throats out—a tough context to overcome.

Context matters in Christian evangelization as well. Take the fellow on the milk crate shouting Bible verses in the park. He's sharing his faith. The context is a public space and his chosen forum makes him an uninvited speaker at best, intrusive at worst. What's the result? Some folks are annoyed, some are amused or intrigued by the phenomenon, and most just walk on by. Over the course of a season, a few souls already harboring troubled consciences may be touched by a random verse, feel personally addressed, and repent their direction. Maybe. But if the guy on the crate does not enjoy the charisma of a Saint Peter or Paul, his success ratio will likely be slim.

Then there's the home-invasion brand of evangelization. I remember a day in college when I was in the dorm crying my eyes out. Someone had broken my heart or whatever. An unexpected knock on the door found me racing to answer it, desperate for a friend, if not the deserter-beloved himself. Instead, I opened the door to someone holding up a brochure, wanting to come in and talk about the End of the World. Livid, I slammed the door in her face. While she was arguably an evangelist, and I apparently in need of good news, neither this woman's arrival nor her tactics were of any use to me on that tear-stained day. I'd put the creep-factor of that encounter up there with the werewolf.

Saint Francis of Assisi originated the phrase: "Preach the gospel at all times. If necessary, use words." That is the guiding principle for effective evangelization. Our faith is a wonderful gift. It's worth spreading far and wide, but that doesn't mean we're obliged to have the "Jesus Talk" with perfect strangers, unless they raise the question. When people share faith with me in ways that genuinely influence me, I take note of how they did it so I can do the same.

How to be a missionary

It helps to have three friends who are real-life missionaries. They're professional faith-spreaders today, but they were "normal" people when I met them. Ken became a Jesuit priest who works as a doctor in parts of Africa that rarely have access to medical care. He provides a vital service that people need, and he does it under really rough circumstances. His life is one big loving sacrifice. But he doesn't say he's doing it for Jesus. He just does it. As a priest, he's already stated with this commitment that Jesus is the reason he's out there.

My friend Mary is a lay social worker with a refugee organization. She served in Bosnia right after the war, assisting Christians and Muslims on both sides of the conflict. She wasn't there to pray with anyone. She was there because people were suffering, and she sees Christ in human suffering. She rarely talks about her motives with the people she's helping. She doesn't have to. Her brave presence in dangerous and difficult places speaks volumes.

Brother John is a Franciscan friar. He studied Russian so he could go to Russia to encourage religious faith in a country that had suppressed its churches for a long time. John's the sort of friendly, happy guy you just want to strike up a conversation with. I can imagine him running around Russia making friends and telling them he's in their country because he loves Jesus so much. I just know Russians would find John so engaging that they'd be curious why Jesus is such a big deal to him and want to hear the whole story.

Let's get this straight: I'm no missionary. I shrink from the idea of leaving my home and doing what my friends are doing; maybe you don't. But I participate in their work by praying for them, as well as supporting the missions financially. I also tell the story of what they're doing to get other people to pray for and support missionaries. That's the first and most obvious way all of us can assist in spreading the gospel around the world.

If supporting missionary work is good, imitating missionaries is better. We can all do what Ken, Mary, and John are doing on our own turf and in the context of our more typical lives. Ken makes sacrifices for the people he serves. He embodies Saint Ignatius of Loyola's ideal of the person who lives for others. Whom do we live for and serve? Family members, friends, fellow parishioners, coworkers, folks in the greater community. How can we serve them sacrificially? By going one step farther than we're inclined to go. Offering forgiveness to those who hurt us before they have to ask. Spending an extra ten minutes listening to someone who needs to talk. Giving up a free night to set up chairs for the parish meeting. Mowing the lawn for the neighbor without a mower.

To imitate what my friend Mary does requires stepping outside my comfort zone. I have to mingle with people who are not like me, don't live as I do, share my values, or talk my religion. I have to be respectful in dialogue, do more listening than talking, refrain from insisting on how others are "wrong" at every bend in the conversation. Respecting someone else's ideas is the best way to gain respect for your own. Whether or not the other person slides over to your position, you've still opened a door, which is a great beginning. I'm not always ready to walk through every door that's been opened for me, but often I do find myself seeing things in a new way as a result of the invitation.

My friend John demonstrates what we usually think of as "real" evangelization: talking to people about Jesus directly. He doesn't do it the "creepy" way—showing up unannounced and unwelcome—but in the context of forming sincere relationships. He meets people where they are and invites the question of faith by presenting the vital testimony of himself. He doesn't pull punches: He's a Franciscan and dresses like one. He's a Jesus guy and he's not afraid to say the Name.

Commitment needed

As a layperson I don't have a uniform that signals the approach of a Catholic—in case anyone prefers to step aside—but I do signal my dedication in other ways. I gather with the faith community at Sunday Mass, dressed in clothes that show I take this event seriously and singularly. My neighbors have learned that I won't eat out or transact any business that makes other people work on this day I so honor. If folks step into my house, they see crosses on the walls, icons of saints, statues of Mary. I carry a rosary, which spills out of my purse when in pursuit of stray items. I've been known to wear a religious medal, I have a t-shirt with my parish's name emblazoned on it, I bless myself when I pass churches, and I bless others when they sneeze. Praying before meals in restaurants, quoting saints in conversation: You can declare your identity as believers without ever pulling out your Catholic card.

So these are some ways we share our faith. Outward displays of religion, though, can be empty signs without a heroic commitment to a Christian life. Following Jesus produces saints. Saint Paul tells us what the fruits of a holy life will be: love, joy, peace, patience, kindness, generosity, faithfulness, gentleness, and self-control (Galatians 5:22-23). Each one of these virtues is a challenge. Taken together they create truly radiant human beings. The kind sure to attract others with the whole-hearted desire to be like them—that is evangelization at its finest.

How to make every Mass count

By Amy Florian

When we gather at Mass, we join others who are also trying to live the gospel as faithful disciples. But there can be some obstacles blocking the Eucharist's power. Here are some simple suggestions to improve your Mass experience.

IMAGINE ATTENDING a birthday party. You arrive to find everyone on couches, pondering their own thoughts and grudgingly moving aside to let others sit. When the birthday person enters, people look up, some smile, and some say a greeting. Yet most remain disconnected. Some share stories, although others don't seem very interested in listening. When "Happy Birthday" begins, only a few (usually those with the best voices) sing wholeheartedly. When gifts are opened, people watch for a while but easily get distracted. Everyone does make sure they get cake, and when the party is finally over, most attendees bolt for the door.

What is the Mass?

Not much of a celebration, right? Yet all too often something similar happens with Mass. The ideal, however, is that the Mass is connected to our lives, and we bring to it the whole of our lives—our doubts, struggles, and suffering as well as our beliefs, hopes, and joys. The Mass is meant to be a celebration that profoundly connects us to the One who can make us whole.

At Mass, we welcome people who might not normally be our friends because the bond of baptism erases divisions. The rich sit by the poor, those with disabilities sit by the able-bodied, the single sit by the married, the jobless sit by the employed, and teens sit by the elderly. Together we listen to the stories that form our identity, our challenges, and our faith. We join together to offer ourselves and our gifts to God, that all may be consecrated as the Body and Blood of Christ. We worship, giving praise and thanks to God for all that we have, and we ask God's protection, guidance, and wisdom for ourselves and our world. We relive the words of Jesus at the Last Supper and wonder in awe as our simple gifts of bread and wine are transformed by God's grace into the actual Body and Blood of Jesus Christ.

Then, though we could never hope to be worthy, we come together to the table of the Lord to receive our incarnate God. In doing so, we become what we receive and are formed ever more into the Body of Christ on earth. Finally, we are sent out to do in the world what we have just done in the liturgy.

If we truly understand the Mass, we understand everything that is important about being a disciple of Christ. This sacrament is a gift, meant to be celebrated, savored, and lived. Unfortunately, though, there can be some obstacles blocking us from this grasp of the Eucharist's power.

The repetition factor

Because the Mass is repeated so often it is easy for people to lapse into over-familiarity or even indifference. After all, we basically know the procedure right down to the final "Amen." Yet what if that were not the case? What if the Mass changed every time? It would be like going to dinner in a restaurant but never knowing in what order the courses would be served, or attending a football game without knowing how many quarters would be played or what rules would be followed. A consistent form is important for participation and for understanding.

Within that framework, though, there are an infinite number of variables. Every time you go to a restaurant or a football game, the experience is different. So is the Mass. On Sundays, we repeat the same readings only once every three years. There are different prayers at each liturgy—even the Eucharistic Prayer has four standard options, three more for children, and two for Reconciliation, plus others for feasts and seasons. The general intercessions are new each week; there are options for the Penitential Rite, and the music is not the same from week to week.

Perhaps more important, though, the Mass is different each time because we are different. The circumstances and events of our lives during that particular week affect our openness to the Spirit, our needs and desires, and our point of contact with God's grace, and that effect is intensified over time.

Imagine, for instance, the experience of liturgy for a 7-year-old First Eucharist candidate, a teenager struggling to find his or her identity, a young married couple with their first child, a middle-aged man reflecting on his life's accomplishments and regrets, and an elderly woman facing terminal illness. No matter how often we celebrate Mass, we are different people each time. That is the beauty of good ritual. It maintains its power through time, even as the people who celebrate it change.

Overcoming obstacles

Sometimes people disengage from Mass because liturgy isn't done well in their parish. That is because our priests and other ministers are first and foremost human beings. The priest may not pray the prayers with much sincerity. His homily may not be inspiring or thought-provoking. The cantor may be slightly off-key or hard to hear clearly. The lector may not proclaim the scripture readings effectively. You can be tempted to sit in the pew and criticize, concentrating on these imperfect ministers.

When you do, though, God's action in you is blocked. It is like the electricity constantly flowing through wires in the walls all around us. We aren't even aware of its power unless we plug in. When a minister is unprepared, instead of bemoaning the ineffective outlet, find another way to plug in. Pray that God will open you to the grace that is there for you.

In addition, remember that there is no "audience" at Mass. Some individuals fill more visible positions, yet every person in every pew has a role in singing, speaking, moving, and actively listening. All too often we come to Mass in a passive frame of mind, expecting to have something done to or for us. But just as poorly prepared ministers can damage the celebration, members of the assembly who aren't well prepared and don't actively participate can render the Mass boring and seemingly motionless.

The power of community

Many people insist they can skip Mass and not miss anything. They say they connect with God by praying in nature or going for a walk. In one sense, they are absolutely right. All creation is filled with the power of God, and we encounter God in varied ways. But is that enough? What happens when crisis or tragedy strikes? In my experience the first thing people do when they receive bad news is grab their phone or computer and reach out to other people.

If I am diagnosed with terminal cancer and arrive at Mass in desperate need of the community but you aren't there, I don't get a chance to receive your support and presence. Then when you are in need, what if I decide to go pray somewhere else instead of being there for you? We are members of a body, and if one part suffers, we all suffer with it. We are created for community, and especially in tough times, the faith community prays for us and sustains us in ways that no one else can.

Nor is it simply personal. These days the news reports are filled with war and violence, scandal and broken trust, disasters and disease. How are we to live justly in the midst of so much injustice? How can we preach forgiveness and reconciliation in a world where vengeance and power are promoted as the way to solve problems? We can only do it together.

Programs such as Alcoholics Anonymous work because they are group efforts in which people support and encourage one another. When we gather at Mass we join with others who are also trying to live the gospel as faithful disciples. As you look around the assembly, you know you are not alone, that you are a member of the one Body with one source and one goal.

We need the Mass as a model of how we are to live the rest of our lives. We should not "go to" Mass solely out of obligation; ideally we celebrate Mass to respond to the One who creates, calls, and saves us, and to receive the grace and nourishment we need to become who we are created to be.

So how can you participate better and improve your Mass experience?

- Learn about liturgy. Read books. Take a class. Understand what we're doing and why.
- Read the scripture passages for the day beforehand. The daily and Sunday readings can be found at www.usccb.org/nab. Notice themes, connections, and especially challenges for your life. Ponder what the homily would be if you were preaching.
- Be welcoming, smiling at people and maybe introducing yourself to someone you don't know. Look at others during Mass, conscious that we are praying together as the Body of Christ.
- Sing with gusto, even if you don't have a stellar voice. Pay attention to the words you are singing, so you can consciously pray them.
- Respond and pray with feeling. When you say "Amen" or "Thanks be to God" or "Lord have mercy," mean it.
- Actively listen through the entire celebration to scripture and the prayers, taking them in and allowing them to affect you.
- Pray that God will use this celebration to open your heart, teach you, and fill you with grace so you may be a better disciple of Christ.

Follow these simple steps and we might all feel like we're at a party this Sunday.

Don't keep from singing

BY FATHER GODFREY MULLEN, O.S.B.

Why do we sing in church? A teacher of liturgy counts the ways.

THE THREE KINGS were coming to my parish on Epiphany, and I was to be the third king, singing my appropriate verse of the song named after the wise and holy trio. It was my first time to sing alone in front of a group. And I was petrified. "Myrrh is mine, its bitter perfume / Breathes a life of gathering gloom; / Sorrowing, sighing, bleeding, dying, / Sealed in the stone-cold tomb." What words for a sixth-grader to sing! But I remember them today, more than 30 years later. When I'm having a day that is less than perfect, I sometimes claim that myrrh again as mine. Those lyrics have stuck with me, partly because the melody was so memorable.

In the church, we have been given the gift of singing as a way of participating in the liturgy. In the church, each member has been given a voice in order to raise a song of thanks and praise to God each and every day. In the church, singing provides the opportunity to welcome God's presence and acclaim God's power. In the church, our singing opens for us a new way to remember God's spoken Word and powerful consolation and God's commands and hopes for us. We sing because God created us to sing, to God's glory and honor. We sing precisely because singing reminds us of God's Word.

In 2007, the United States Conference of Catholic Bishops issued their most recent document on liturgical music, titled *Sing to the Lord: Music in Divine Worship*. In it they ask: Why do we sing?

God is present

"When His people sing, God is present among them" (*Sing to the Lord*, no. 1). Having gathered in the name of the Trinity, we know God is present in our midst (Matthew 18:20). When we lend our voices to the communal voice of the church, we can be all the more certain that our singing acclaims the beauty of God. From the psalms of old to inspiring sacred music of our own time, we are given melodies and lyrics to sing so that God's presence might rightly be acknowledged. We sing in gratitude for God's everlasting presence.

Sing to spread faith

"Singing makes the melodies of our faith accessible to others" (*Sing*, no. 2). Hum a few bars of "Jingle Bells" or "Happy Birthday" in a room full of people and watch the effect. The happiness of our own hearts, the faith that wells up from our souls, the joy of our worship overflows from within us and spreads to those around us.

Singing what we believe and, even more important, singing the Word of God handed on to us, we are privileged to let others access the tradition that has shaped and sustained us. Music can become a wonderful tool for evangelization in each believer's life, especially when music seems so pervasive in our culture. The message becomes more accessible to more people as they hear and remember some ancient truth of faith sung in a melody that touches them to the core. We sing to spread the Word of God to others.

Sing for strength

"This common, sung expression of faith within liturgical celebrations strengthens our faith when it grows weak and draws us into the divinely inspired voice of the church at prayer" (*Sing*, no. 5). The discipline of communal prayer, especially the Liturgy of the Hours, calls the Christian faithful to pray however they may feel. That discipline moves individuals to join the communal voice, transfiguring individual efforts by the light of the community's praise of God.

The Liturgy of the Hours is another opportunity for the one praying to remember the intentions of all the church but also the honor of speaking the Word of God for those who do not have the ability, the time, or the opportunity to pray the church's public prayer. And so the commitment to this regular prayer can be a genuine sacrifice when it is difficult and can be an authentic source of strength when our faith or morale lags. We sing for strength when we are weak. We sing to support the harmonious voice of the Body of Christ.

Sing your faith in the Resurrection

The basic melody of the liturgy is a "canticle of victory over sin and death" (*Sing*, no. 7). Not unlike the strengthening of weakened faith, the undying lyrics of the liturgy are the song of the Resurrection. Sung first by the women at the tomb and taken up later by the other disciples, the joy of Easter is sung in the hearts of Christian believers because life has conquered death, once and for all, yesterday, today, and forever. Regardless of the type or weight of the cross we may be carrying today, the paschal tune of hope plays through our living. We sing to inspire hope in the resurrection.

Sing to do God's work

"Charity, justice, and evangelization are the result of liturgical celebration" (*Sing*, no. 9). Just as singing is so central to the work of the church, it creates a memory that reminds us of an ethical commitment to life that Catholics have, particularly having celebrated the Eucharist. The liturgy, the church's source of all power and the summit toward which all its work is aimed, calls for music that creates memory for us. As our memory is shaped by our regular encounter with the Christian peace that we experience in the liturgy, it rises up within us when the decisions of daily living are less clear.

We sing a memory of myrrh that refuses to end up only in the stable, on the cross, or in the grave but also in an empty tomb. We sing a memory of fearlessness when we join the psalm: "The Lord is my light and my salvation, of whom should I be afraid?" We sing a memory of stability when the words of the hymn spill out of us: "The church's one foundation is Jesus Christ her Lord." And these memories stand as a clarion call to a life of charity and justice, the work of all Christ's followers as we spread his gospel. We sing to remind ourselves of the light we've promised to live every time we go to Mass.

Why we sing

In the end, we are moved to song because God is present. We sing that the faith might spread. We sing for our own strength and the strength of the church's voice. We sing because of our faith in the Resurrection. We sing for accountability in the Christian life. We sing because God gave us mouths and voices, hearts and minds to remember God's Word and words about God in the beautiful and memorable melodies of God's beloved people. We sing to God. We sing for us.

Faith and everyday life

BY LAWRENCE CUNNINGHAM

Being a Christian means adopting a certain way of life, and spirituality is living the Christian life in the concrete situation where we find ourselves.

SPIRITUALITY IS A BUZZWORD today, and it covers many things. Spirituality for some people means gazing into crystals, for others it means 12-step programs. Sometimes my students say that they are spiritual but not religious or they believe in spirituality but they don't believe in religion.

I am going to focus on the notion of spirituality with the adjective Christian, and even that is a difficult phrase to identify. In a recent book I wrote, I have an appendix in the first chapter that lists 28 different definitions of Christian spirituality. But for our purposes, I am simply going to describe spirituality as living the Christian life in the concrete situation in which we find ourselves. In that sense Christian living will have different emphases depending on who we are. As Saint Francis de Sales put it in the opening pages of his classic work *Introduction to the Devout Life*, "a devotion which conflicts with anyone's state of life is undoubtedly false."

A certain way of life

Let me start off with something rather contentious: Being a Christian does not mean accepting on faith a certain number of ideas or doctrines abstractly put or moral teachings or codes of conduct. Being a Christian means to adopt a certain way of life, and I am going to put my emphasis on the word *way*.

In the New Testament the earliest recorded name of the followers of Jesus was that they were followers of the way. Saint Paul, in the Acts of the Apostles, says that before he was converted he was a persecutor "of the way." Being Christian is a way of life—and a way of discipleship. The word *disciple* occurs 250 times in the New Testament. Of those 250 times, 70 times the word is linked to some form of the word *follow*. To be a disciple is to be a follower.

The fundamental basis for being a Christian is to become a disciple of the living Jesus, to learn of him, what he stands for, what he has done, what he has promised, and how in following him you become a new kind of person. Being a Christian means to adopt a certain way of life, and that way of life is the way of discipleship.

Commitment to that way of discipleship

Every kind of discipleship demands a commitment; it does not come instantly. That is why we call this way of discipleship a way of life. It takes time and experience, failure and success, joy and discouragement, to advance as a disciple. That is pretty clear from the New Testament where even those who were closest to Jesus didn't always understand what he was talking about. Indeed, the Gospel of John over and over again says it was not until the time of the Resurrection that they understood what Jesus fully meant. If the way of discipleship, this way of life is one that demands growth, it simply means that Christians must grow in maturity.

Growth in this way of discipleship with Jesus is a process by which we can learn from those who have gone before us. The Letter to the Hebrews talks about a cloud of witnesses, the people who are with us now and who have gone before us, some of whom we celebrate as saints. We have an enormous tradition that stands behind the Catholic tradition that helps us to understand the way of discipleship, yet not everybody is called to every way of discipleship.

We all believe the basic creed and worship in the same liturgy and observe the same moral life, but the ways in which we can mature as Christians are many. If you like your religious practice to be exuberant, we have ways of being exuberant. If you like to follow the poor Jesus, we have the Franciscan tradition. If you want to follow the Jesus who spends the night in prayer, we have the contemplative tradition. The point is that in the paths of maturity we don't have to invent the Christian life over and over again. What we need to do is find those resources that help us to understand what it means to be a follower of Jesus.

Christian life in the coming millennium

What is the new millennium going to bring us as Catholic Christians? The church in the new millennium will do the same thing it has done in the past two millennia: It will gather the community, it will invite others to join, it will tell the saving story of Christ, and it will break the bread. That was the task of the church in its beginnings, it is its task now, and it will be its task in the future. Paul tells us in his letter to the Corinthians that we will break the bread until the Lord comes again. What is going to be interesting in the new millennium is to ask the question, "How is that story going to be told? And how is that bread going to be broken?"

Second, Christians of the future, the theologian Karl Rahner once wrote, will either be mystics or not Christian at all. Rahner saw rather clearly that this kind of Catholicism he knew growing up, of a close-knit community with common values, was disappearing under the forces of secularization, urbanization, and other factors.

The point that Rahner was trying to make was that in the future people were either going to have to be committed to the Christian faith by experience or they would not be Christians at all simply because there would be no cultural pay-offs; the culture was not going to support the idea of being a Christian. In our country today, people are still vigorous churchgoers. It always amazes Europeans to come to this country and discover how much Christians still value churches and support religion. But in this country, there has also been a shift away from the cultural model about which Rahner was speaking.

So the new question is: Do we today have the resources, and do we have the understanding, to allow people to be deeply experiential in their faith in order to sustain them in a culture that in this country is not hostile but largely indifferent to religious values?

Third, Christians of the future will have to take into account, if they want to be a vital part of the human community, the simple, observable fact that our culture is becoming increasingly pluralistic. There are dramatic shifts taking place all over the Western world. The second largest religious tradition in France today is Muslim. You can go to any city in America today and see this religious pluralism. What does that say about the future of Christian values and how these values are going to be understood? If the church is going to be a voice, it's going to have to take into account this radical religious pluralism.

Pope John Paul II in his encyclical *Redemptoris Missio* said that just as Saint Paul had to go to the Areopagus—the main square of Athens—to speak about the gospel in terms the Athenians would understand, so today we have a new areopagus, we have a new playing field, we have a new audience today we have to speak to. How is the language of the gospel made sense of amid the many competing voices of the pluralism of opinions, the pluralism of ideas, the pluralism of cultures in the interconnected world in which we live?

Fourth, we are living today through the greatest communications revolution since Johannes Gutenberg's 15th-century invention of movable type in the West, which radically changed the communication system in Europe. Books became inexpensive and could be put in the hands of everyone, which led to a rise in literacy and a thirst for reading material. Human beings lived in a book culture ever since then until the 20th century when we began to have radio and television. But today, in the age of computers, cheap televisions, and cellular networks, what is the future of preaching the gospel going to be in those circumstances? In many ways, the church today is riding a horse and buggy, while the communications industry is moving in a sports car, and we haven't understood the full implications of this gap.

Crisis and opportunity?

There are many problems facing the church in the new millennium. You could even say it's a crisis—but in Chinese, the character for crisis means both "danger" and "opportunity." We have to ask how well we communicate the gospel in this new world. If the world asks for bread, let's be sure we are giving them bread and not a stone.

Contributors *(in alphabetical order)*

FATHER BRITTO M. BERCHMANS is pastor of St. Paul of the Cross church in Park Ridge, Illinois.

FATHER PAUL BOUDREAU is a priest of the Diocese of Norwich, Connecticut. He is coauthor with Alice Camille of *The Forgiveness Book,* available from ACTA Publications.

ALICE CAMILLE is an author and religious educator. She is author of *Invitation to Catholicism* (ACTA Publications), *Listening to God's Word* (Orbis Books), *The Rosary: Mysteries of Joy, Light, Sorrow, and Glory* (ACTA Publications), and other titles. She is a regular contributor to "Questions Catholics ask," a featured column on the VISION Vocation Network, VocationNetwork. org, and writes the monthly "Exploring the Word" column for *Prepare the Word* (TrueQuest Communications).

KEVIN CLARKE is a senior editor and chief correspondent of *America* magazine.

LAWRENCE CUNNINGHAM is the John A. O'Brien Professor of Theology at the University of Notre Dame. His article is adapted from a lecture he gave as part of Notre Dame's Satellite Theological Education Program (STEP), which offers online theological education and faith formation opportunities to adult Catholics across the country.

AMY FLORIAN is a liturgy and bereavement consultant living in Illinois. She has published numerous articles and two books and is nationally known as a speaker, retreat director, and teacher.

SISTER SUSAN ROSE FRANCOIS, C.S.J.P. is a member of the Sisters of St. Joseph of Peace. She is on the staff of the Intercommunity Peace and Justice Center in Seattle.

BRYAN FROEHLE is professor of practical theology and director of the Ph.D. Program in Practical Theology at St. Thomas University, Miami Gardens, Florida.

SISTER SUSAN KIDD, C.N.D. is a Congregation of Notre Dame Sister. She has served as vocation director for English Canada, was a missionary in Cameroon, and now works at the University of Prince Edward Island in Atlantic Canada as a campus minister.

CATHERINE LOFTUS, a graduate of St. Ignatius College Prep in Chicago, is currently a student at the University of Michigan.

JOHN W. MARTENS is associate professor of theology at the University of St. Thomas in St. Paul, Minnesota and director of the master's in theology program at the St. Paul Seminary School of Divinity. He writes "The Word" column for *America* magazine.

FATHER JAMES MARTIN, S.J. is a Jesuit priest, author, and editor at large of *America*. His books include *Jesus: A Pilgrimage* (HarperOne), *Between Heaven and Mirth* (HarperOne), and *My Life with the Saints* (Loyola Press).

PAT MORRISON writes from Ohio. In conjunction with her travels as a journalist, she has made pilgrimages in Italy, the Holy Land, and early Christian martyrdom sites in Tunisia. A vowed laywoman in the Carmelite tradition, she is a member of the Association of Contemplative Sisters.

STEVE MUELLER is an author, speaker, teacher, and editor of the quarterly publication *Words of Grace: Daily Reflections & Prayers for Catholics* (All Saints Press).

FATHER GODFREY MULLEN, O.S.B. is a Benedictine monk of St. Meinrad Archabbey in St. Meinrad, Indiana. Vice rector of Saint Meinrad Seminary and School of Theology, he also teaches liturgy there and is interim manager of One Bread, One Cup, an annual liturgical conference for high school youth and campus and youth ministers.

LINUS MUNDY is former director of publications at Abbey Press and the founder of two of their popular booklets series, *CareNotes* and *PrayerNotes*. He has also written numerous articles for the religious press as well as books on the Desert Elders, Saint Benedict, and the art of slowing down and keeping life simple.

SEAN REYNOLDS is a graduate of Saint Xavier University with a B.A. in English currently pursuing his doctorate at SUNY Buffalo.

FATHER RONALD ROLHEISER, O.M.I., theologian, teacher, and award-winning author, is president of the Oblate School of Theology in San Antonio, Texas.

FATHER DONALD SENIOR, C.P. is a Passionist priest, president of Catholic Theological Union in Chicago, professor of New Testament studies. A member of the Pontifical Biblical Commission, he is general editor of the Catholic Study Bible (Oxford University Press) and author of the four-volume *The Passion of Jesus in the Gospels of Mark, Matthew, Luke, and John* (Michael Glazier/Liturgical Press). His article was adapted from an address Father Senior gave at the 2008 Convocation of the National Religious Vocation Conference (NRVC) in Louisville, Kentucky.

BROTHER DAVID STEINDL-RAST, O.S.B. is a Benedictine monk, an author and lecturer, and the cofounder of gratefulness.org.

PATRICE J. TUOHY is co-founder and publisher of TrueQuest Communications, publishers of *Prepare the Word* and *Take Five for Faith*, and executive editor of *VISION Vocation Guide*, a publication of the National Religious Vocation Conference.

Other resources available from TrueQuest Communications:

Prepare the Word: Whole Parish Evangelization, *PrepareTheWord.com*

Take Five for Faith: Daily Renewal for Busy Catholics, *TakeFiveForFaith.com*

Questions Catholics Ask, available at *PrepareTheWord.com* and *VocationNetwork.org*

About TrueQuest Communications

TrueQuest Communications is a Chicago-based Catholic publishing company that serves the needs of spiritual seekers, religious communities, parishes, and faith-based organizations through thoughtful, high-quality publications and expert publishing and communication services.

TrueQuest's award-winning publications include *Prepare the Word: Whole Parish Evangelization, Take Five for Faith: Daily Renewal for Busy Catholics,* and *VISION Vocation Guide,* which is published by TrueQuest on behalf of the National Religious Vocation Conference.

For more information about TrueQuest Communications and its publications and services, visit *TrueQuestWeb.com*.